A Guide to The Good Life: Insight from Ecclesiastes
© 2013 by Midtown Fellowship. All rights reserved.
ISBN 978-0-9899441-0-6 (paperback)
Published by Midtown Fellowship

All rights reserved. No part of this book may be reproduced or utilized in any form or by any means, electronic or mechanical, or by any information storage and retrieval system—except for brief quotations for the purpose of review, without written permission from the publisher.

Scripture taken from THE ENGLISH STANDARD VERSION. ©2001 by Crossway Bibles, a division of Good News Publishers.

CONTENTS

Introduction	5
Weekly Plan	11

SECTION 1: STUDY GUIDES

1: The Treadmill	17
2: The Experiment	37
3: The Trophy Case	55
4: The Illusion of Control	77
5: Flyin' Solo	95
6: The Champagne Club	115
7: The Fountain of Youth	135
8: Joy, Satisfaction & the Fear of God	149

SECTION 2: DEVOTIONALS

Introduction	169
Reading Schedule	171

SECTION 3: FAMILY GUIDE

Introduction	215
Family Activities	219
Family Devotionals	227
Prayer Guides	253

APPENDICES

A: The Solomon Club	273
B: Interpretive Difficulties	285
C: Extra Resources	291

INTRODUCTION

"I hope everybody could get rich and famous and will have everything they ever dreamed of, so they will know that it's not the answer."

- Jim Carrey

In some ways, the quality of life in America has never been better. A surprising amount of research is beginning to show that over the last fifty years almost every factor in quality of life has improved.[1] And at the same time, no one seems to be getting happier. We are all chasing the good life and in some ways we are achieving circumstantially the good life at higher rates than ever before. And at the same time, depression and anxiety are up.[2] Happiness is down.[3]

Enter Ecclesiastes.

No one in human history has lived an affluent, glamorous lifestyle more fully than Solomon. No one has had more cumulative wealth, wisdom, success, power, and rampant access to anything he wanted whenever he wanted it. And somehow his conclusion was even massive increases in wealth, success, and overall quality of life

---

1 Reference Gregg Easterbrook's *The Progress Paradox. How Life Gets Better While People Feel Worse* (New York City, NY: Random House Trade Paperbacks, 2004).
2 Anxiety and depression have greatly increased at every age level over the past 30-50 years. For more information, **go to www.midtowncolumbia.com/GoodLifeLinks link #2.**
3 As noted in Gregg Easterbrook's *The Progress Paradox... How Life Gets Better While People Feel Worse* (New York City, NY: Random House Trade Paperbacks, 2004). Also consider this interesting article in which the social media website Twitter has observed a decline in the overall happiness of it's tweets. **Go to www.midtowncolumbia.com/GoodLifeLinks link #3.** (http://www.mediabistro.com/alltwitter/global-happiness-is-declining-at-least-on-twitter_b17052)

do not translate to deep-down, soul level satisfaction and joy.

Which means Solomon's got some insight for our culture.

Solomon was chasing everything we chase thousands of years before us.

And he's already finished the race so he can now look back and bless us with his conclusions in hindsight. The entire book of Ecclesiastes is Solomon saying, "Let me tell you what I have already learned is the inevitable end of everything you are chasing right now."

So as an entire church family, we are going to allow Solomon's ancient insight and wisdom – wisdom that has stood the test of time – to enlighten us in our modern pursuits of the good life. Throughout the next eight weeks we will sync up our Sunday Gatherings, Kidtown lessons, and LifeGroups to study through some of the major themes of the book of Ecclesiastes.

At times you are going to feel like Solomon needs a hug. His analysis is razor sharp, but his tone is at times less-than-chipper. The reason for Solomon's apparent pessimism is directly related to the nature of the task he is accomplishing. Throughout the book, Solomon bounces back and forth in a tension of two opposite views of life:

Life with no view of God.

Life with God in view.

Solomon spends a majority of his time considering the first view. This is what he refers to as life "under the sun" (appears twenty-seven times throughout the book) and it is also why it often feels like Solomon forgot to take his Prozac. By zooming his view primarily in on the human experience without God in view, Solomon illuminates much of the underlying hollowness and darkness of secular life. Over and over, his observations of life with no view of God return him to his conclusion that life is meaningless. "Vanity of vanities."[4] The Hebrew word *hebel* used here is interchangeably translated as vanity, vapor, nothing or meaningless.

Nothing of nothingness.

It's important to note that this frequently repeated theme is not Solomon's actual conclusion on life, but only his conclusion on life with no view of God. The brief moments when Solomon points our attention "beyond the sun" arrive as breaths of fresh air throughout the book. Despite the fact that some of his conclusions can seem absolutely depressing, he consistently returns to the same conclusion: God gives us great resting places to enjoy Him and His gifts throughout life's journey. However, He does not permit us to mistake a sin-cursed world for our final home. Put another way, God is begging us to escape being trapped in life under the sun and to catch some of His eternal perspective. Until we do so, we will never enjoy fully all God has to offer us in the here and now, or in eternity that is to come.

Put even more simply, without God, we never find the good life.

We are very excited about looking at some of the major themes Solomon touches on throughout this campaign. Ecclesiastes, when understood properly, contains an ocean's worth of wisdom to protect us like a moat from the siren calls of materialism, secularism, individualism, idealism, and performancism. These perspectives are the air we breathe in our culture. We are praying Jesus will use this study to grow our family in loving Him, living in light of eternity with Him, and learning to help our neighbors, friends, and family see the vanity of living life without Jesus in view.

Please join us in praying for our family throughout this study:

- Pray Jesus will give us deep, honest insight into the underlying emptiness of many of the things we are chasing after to give us the good life.

---

[4] Ecclesiastes 1:2

- Pray Jesus will give us more of His perspective from beyond the sun.
- Pray we will grow as missionaries who can help discern and explain the deep down broken emptiness of life that many of our neighbors and friends are experiencing.
- Pray Jesus will help our city see our need for Him in order to live the good life.
- Pray Jesus will rescue us from the trap of individualism and help us live heavily intertwined, mutually encouraging lives as a church family.
- Pray Jesus will protect us from the temptation of materialism and performancism and help us find our identity is perfectly given to us as a gift in Him.
- Pray we will grow in contentment, enjoyment, and experiencing of the good life found in Jesus.

In our most expansive campaign to date, we are offering you three separate sections in this book to serve you, your LifeGroup and your family. The first section is a weekly study and discussion guide (much like what we have published in previous campaigns: *A Marriage You'd Actually Want* and *Outlier**). The second section is a more personal and in depth study for those of you who would like to study deeper. It includes a reading plan to help you read the entire book of Ecclesiastes during the eight weeks of this campaign and personal daily devotions to help you meditate and digest the wisdom of Ecclesiastes in light of the gospel. The third section contains a Family Guide to help parents lead their family in studying the book of Ecclesiastes and learning to love Jesus more. Kidtown will be syncing up with the Gatherings and studying through Ecclesiastes along side of us. The Family Guide will give you a way to connect what you are learning with what your kids are learning.

In all of this, our goal is to help you love Jesus and center your entire life on His unbelievable grace and love for you. How beautiful would it be for Jesus' grace to use Solomon's ancient wisdom to help us better understand our modern, advanced world? How beautiful would it be for Jesus to expose and set us free from baited traps in our worldview that incapacitate our ability to live the good life? How beautiful would it be for Jesus to use Ecclesiastes to help us live in light of and speak the gospel more effectively to our neighbors and our friends and family?

We love you and we are praying for you.

We are excited to see Jesus invite us into His good life.[5]

---

[5] John 10:10

WEEKLY PLAN

SEPTEMBER 22: THE TREADMILL
ECCLESIASTES 1
Under the sun, life is boring, monotonous, and repetitive if you don't understand spiritual reality in light of Jesus who gives meaning to everything. Jesus entered into life under the sun to rescue us from the rut of boring, repetitive selfishness in which we find ourselves trapped. Jesus alone can fill our lives with ultimate meaning and purpose because ultimate meaning and purpose belong to Him.

SEPTEMBER 29: THE EXPERIMENT
ECCLESIASTES 2:1-17
King Solomon engages in a soul-searching experiment; he tests every common pursuit in life and every way of looking at life to see if he can find lasting meaning or satisfaction. His conclusion is no matter what lens you look through, no matter what you pursue, without spiritual, eternal perspective, everything fails to deliver what it promises and you die having wasted your life.

NOVEMBER 6: THE TROPHY CASE
ECCLESIASTES 2:18-26
Most people frolic through childhood enjoying responsibility free pleasure for the first 18-25ish years of their life. At this point, a

magic switch turns on and most decide, "That was fun, now I need to grow up. I need to get a job, build some-thing, have a family, settle down and make something of my life." The problem is this building and accomplishing mentality often turns into a crippling and self-defeating performancism with no lasting ability to give us life.

OCTOBER 13: THE ILLUSION OF CONTROL
ECCLESIASTES 3:1-15

Solomon's reflection on the seasons of life in Ecclesiastes chapter 3 provided us with two great things: a #1 hit song by the Byrds in 1965 and a complete dismantling of the insane illusion we are in control of our lives. God controls the ingredients and the seasons of our lives and His intention in all of these ingredients is to shape us for His glory and our joy.

OCTOBER 20: FLYIN' SOLO
ECCLESIASTES 4:1-16

In America, individualism is the air we breathe, the food we eat and the way we protect ourselves from any authority or community that wants any say in the decisions we make. The problem with this is God designed us to live heavily intertwined lives where we love one another, serve one another, share life with one another and rely on one another. Solomon exposes the bitter foolishness of being so individualistic that you would fly solo, fall solo and die solo.

OCTOBER 27: THE CHAMPAGNE CLUB
ECCLESIASTES 5:8-20

In a culture where industrial production vastly supersedes required consumption, marketing gurus stopped selling us their products and started selling us a need for their product. The result is we don't buy products we actually need. We buy products that give us status. We don't drive a car; we drive an image. We don't wear an outfit; we wear cloth billboards proclaiming our coolness to the world. Once again, Grandpa Solomon steps in to help us see we don't exist to purchase, consume, or own items. We exist to be owned by Jesus and to receive His status, His image, and His value.

NOVEMBER 3: THE FOUNTAIN OF YOUTH
ECCLESIASTES 9:1-10

Death terrifies us. Every wrinkle, every grey hair, every sag, and ache and tweak sends shivers up our spines. This is clearly evidenced by the fact that the anti-aging industry is set to rake in $115 billion dollars/year by 2015. For thousands of years, cultures all over the world have told stories of the fountain of youth, a mystical way to cheat the inevitability of death. But Solomon encourages us to embrace the reality that death is coming for all of us no matter what we do. Facing our fatal fear drives us to our need for Jesus' help now and in the afterlife.

NOVEMBER 10: JOY, SATISFACTION AND THE FEAR OF GOD
ECCLESIASTES 11:8-12:14

To summarize our study of Ecclesiastes, we'll land on Solomon's parting wisdom. "Fear God and keep his commandments, for this is the whole duty of man." Don't postpone your pursuit of God. Don't wait until the end of your life to realize all your experimental pursuits were meaningless. Find life beyond the sun now and let Jesus fill every aspect of your life with His joy, meaning and purpose.

SECTION ONE
STUDY GUIDES

The words of the Preacher, the son of David, king in Jerusalem. Vanity of vanities, says the Preacher, vanity of vanities! All is vanity. What does man gain by all the toil at which he toils under the sun? A generation goes, and a generation comes, but the earth remains forever. The sun rises, and the sun goes down, and hastens to the place where it rises. The wind blows to the south and goes around to the north; around and around goes the wind, and on its circuits the wind returns. All streams run to the sea, but the sea is not full; to the place where the streams flow, there they flow again. All things are full of weariness; a man cannot utter it; the eye is not satisfied with seeing, nor the ear filled with hearing. What has been is what will be, and what has been done is what will be done, and there is nothing new under the sun. Is there a thing of which it is said, "See, this is new?" It has been already in the ages before us. There is no remembrance of former things, nor will there be any remembrance of later things yet to be among those who come after.

I the Preacher have been king over Israel in Jerusalem. And I applied my heart to seek and to search out by wisdom all that is done under heaven. It is an unhappy business that God has given to the children of man to be busy with. I have seen everything that is done under the sun, and behold, all is vanity and a striving after wind. What is crooked cannot be made straight, and what is lacking cannot be counted. I said in my heart, "I have acquired great wisdom, surpassing all who were over Jerusalem before me, and my heart has had great experience of wisdom and knowledge." And I applied my heart to know wisdom and to know madness and folly. I perceived that this also is but a striving after wind. For in much wisdom is much vexation, and he who increases knowledge increases sorrow.

Ecclesiastes 1:1-18

CHAPTER ONE

THE TREADMILL

CHASING THE GOOD LIFE

Every single one of us is trying to live the good life. Whether we are consciously putting effort and strategy into it, or just winging it and taking life as it comes to us, none of us are attempting to lose at the game of life. None of us are thinking to ourselves, "I sure hope I go about life in the dumbest, most painful way possible."

The desire to enjoy, chase, and win at life is self-evident.

And it's backed up by cultural evidence everywhere.

The self-help industry is raking in around $11 billion a year.[6]

John LaRosa, the research director for The U.S. Market For Self-Improvement Products & Services, explains: "There is no shortage of demand for products and programs that cater to Americans' desire to make more money, lose weight, improve their relationships and business skills, cope with stress, or obtain a quick dose of motivation."

We want to help ourselves live the good life.

The counseling industry is racking in around $14 billion a year.[7]

---

6 **Go to www.midtowncolumbia.com/GoodLifeLinks link #6.**
7 IBIS World's IBIS World's report studied psychologists, social workers and marriage counselors and found 5% increase in each of the five years leading up to 2013. It also anticipates 5% increase in each of the five years coming after 2013. This doesn't include life coaches, credit counselors, financial counselors or personal trainers. For more information, **go to www.midtowncolumbia.com/GoodLifeLinks link #7.**

We want other people to help us live the good life.
The melody plays in marketing campaigns.
Groupon challenges us to "Banish boredom."[8]
Jaguar asks us, "How alive are you?"[9]
Pepsi encouraged us to "Do Good."[10]
Marketers manipulate us through our desire to live the good life.
Even political campaigns get in on this longing inside us.
Obama told us, "Yes we can!"[11]
Whether you agree with his ideas or not...
Whether you think he's the worst or greatest president ever...
Either way, he sold voters on hope...
Hope that we can live the good life.
It's a powerfully compelling idea.

> How successfully do you think you are living the good life? What would you need for your life to be more satisfying? What are your goals? What is your ideal or dream life?
>
> _____
>
> _____
>
> _____
>
> _____
>
> What would change if you got the ideal life you've always dreamed of? Do you think you would move

---

8 Groupon is a web based social couponing company that recommends fun restaurants and entertainment options at a discounted price.
9 Jaguar Motors USA started this campaign to advertise for the sporty XJ "machines". **Go to www.midtowncolumbia.com/GoodLifeLinks link #9.**
10 For the 2010 SuperBowl, Pepsi decided to forego their SuperBowl advertisements and donate $20 million dollars to cause-oriented, fan-submitted do-good projects.
11 Obama's 2007 presidential campaign brought him from less than 10% brand recognition to the highest total money raising political campaign the world has ever seen.

on to wanting something else or would you be content and satisfied?

_____

_____

_____

_____

Solomon has some incredible insight for our pursuit of the good life. In the first two chapters of Ecclesiastes he starts with his conclusion (ch. 1) and his process (ch. 2). Solomon's process is one of the most amazing experiments ever performed in human history; one we all wish we could be a part of. He pursues anything and everything in life with almost unlimited resources. But before he tells us about the experiment in more detail, first he gives us his conclusions:

"'Vanity of vanities', says the Preacher, 'Vanity of vanities! All is vanity.'"[12]

Everything I sought out in all of human experience.

Turned out to be vain.

Empty.

Meaningless.

This is a rough sounding conclusion for our optimistically tuned modern ears. But Solomon's goal isn't to depress us. And fortunately for us, he's willing to help us out by showing us his work.

STUCK IN A CYCLE

Read Ecclesiastes 1:4-7. What strikes Solomon as he observes the natural world we live in? What do you think Solomon is trying to tell us? Where have you seen repetitious cycles in your life?

_____

_____

_____

_____

Solomon is not trying to give us an eighth grade science lesson. He's using weather and natural science to expose the repetitive nature of life. From the rotation of the earth and the sun coursing through the sky, to the jet stream and the water cycle, everything in nature circles back on itself with no seeming end.

It's almost like nature is mocking us.

Taunting us.

Reflecting back to us the boring repetition of our own lives.

Solomon thinks nature is trying to tell us something...

For all of our effort, we're not really getting anywhere.

This shows up at a simple level in really shallow and mundane tasks in our lives. In 2005, author and professor David Foster Wallace delivered a commencement speech at Kenyon College, in which he spoke with great clarity about this issue. *Before you keep reading, you should go watch it by following the instructions in the footnote.*[13]

In the commencement address, Wallace explains: "There happen to be whole, large parts of adult American life that nobody talks about in commencement speeches. One such part involves boredom, routine and petty frustration."

He goes on to describe a typical day in the normal life of an average adult human being:

"You get up in the morning, and go to your challenging job, and you work hard for eight or ten hours, and at the end of the day

---

13 **Go to www.midtowncolumbia.com/GoodLifeLinks link #13.**

you're tired and stressed and all you want is to go home, eat supper, and hit the sack early because you have to do it all again the next day.

... But then you remember there's no food at home...

You haven't had time to shop because of your challenging job, so you have to drive to the supermarket. It's the end of the day and the traffic is very bad, so getting to the store takes longer than it should. The supermarket is very crowded, because all the other people with jobs are also trying to squeeze in some grocery shopping.

You can't just get in and out; you have to wander through confusing aisles and you have to maneuver through other tired, hurried people and eventually you get your supplies, except there aren't enough checkout lanes open. So the checkout line is incredibly long, which is stupid and infuriating. But you can't take your frustration out on the frantic lady working the register, who is overworked and whose daily meaninglessness surpasses the imagination of any of us . . .

But you finally pay for your food, and you get told to "Have a nice day" in a voice that is the absolute voice of death..."

> Have you ever experienced these kinds of moments in life? What feelings and memories rise up in you as he describes this mundane, average day in an adult human's life?
>
> _____
> _____
> _____
> _____

Wallace concludes his honest description by noting that monotonous, infuriating moments like a traffic-filled trip to the grocery store are part of "actual life routine, day after week after month after year... And many more dreary, annoying, seemingly meaningless routines besides."

It's almost like Professor Wallace had been reading and meditating on Solomon's words in the first chapter of Ecclesiastes. His observation that life is full of dreary, annoying, meaningless routines directly echoes Solomon's theme that "all is vanity... all things are full of weariness."[14]

Even the passing generations of humanity bring no real lasting change:

History repeats itself.

Though it's an old cliché, have you ever thought about why it's an old cliché?

It's an old cliché because it's true.

History *does* repeat itself over and over again.

Have you noticed it in your own life?

Have you noticed it in the world around you?

It's like humanity is stuck on a treadmill.

And not just in terms of fashion trends and architectural style. Human generations form an inescapable cycle from birth to adolescence to maturity to retirement to death where we hand everything we've accomplished to the next generation. And the next generation takes over, excitedly coursing through the exact same cycle. Have you ever seen children turn into their parents? Have you ever seen a parent say that thing to their kids they promised they would never say?

Solomon is helping us see that for all our effort we're not really getting anywhere. We're stuck. Like Wallace's blunt words, Solomon strips some of the rhetorical niceties away and asks us the daunting question, "What's the point?"

---

[14] Ecclesiastes 1:2 and 8

"What does a man gain from all the toil at which he toils under the sun?"

Seriously, what is the point of all of this?
Have you ever thought about it?
All this dreary, annoying, meaningless routine?
What's the point of sitting in traffic again?
Do I really have to wash this dish again?
Doesn't this movie have the exact same plot as the last Die Hard?[15]

In a million tiny and larger ways we are stuck.

Because as much as we might fight it, there exist certain cycles of human existence from which you and I cannot escape. In his commentary on Ecclesiastes, William P. Brown notes:

> "The whole world is a scene of incessant movement and activity. But is it purposeful?... For all the constant motion that characterizes the cosmos, one would think that something is being accomplished. But no. Even as the millennia come and go, any semblance of progress is only a mirage. Activity abounds; everything is in perpetual motion, like a hamster in a wheel, but no destination is reached. This display of endless cosmic exertion is all for naught."[16]

Sidney Greidanus adds to Brown's explanation, "In human history too, we see frantic activity but it is not going anywhere. All we see is futile repetition. 'What has been done is what will be done.'"[17] There are repetitious patterns in our lives we simply can't dodge,

---

15 The Die Hard series of movies has currently produced 5 movies with a sixth movie in production, because that story has not yet been fully told my friends. Many action movies have almost identically copied the Die Hard plots. For examples check out Dredd, Olympus Has Fallen and White House Down.
16 Brown, William P. *Ecclesiastes* (Louisville, KY: John Knox, 2000) p. 23.
17 Greidanus, Sydney. *Preaching Christ from Ecclesiastes* (Grand Rapids, MI: Wm. B. Eedmans Publishing Co., 2010) p. 46.

neglect or run from.

> What would you say is the purpose of all the "incessant movement and activity" in creation? In what ways have you noticed "incessant movement and activity" in your life that doesn't seem very purposeful?

_____

_____

_____

_____

ARE OUR SOLUTIONS WORKING?

> **Read Ecclesiastes 1:9-11.** Why do you think Solomon tells us there is nothing new and nothing will be remembered? How do you agree or disagree with his observation?

_____

_____

_____

_____

In many forms and arenas, we try to find ways out of the cycle of life: from numbing ourselves through entertainment, to thrill seeking for the latest adrenaline rush or traveling to new places of grandiose landscapes and amazing relaxation.

Some of us look to fantasy escapes in the expansive literary world of books.

Many of us look to video games and virtual reality to give us a new, exciting battle, mission or purpose in life.

Even shopping, acquiring and collecting give our souls this weird feeling something will be different now. The last time you got something new, what kind of excitement did you feel? Was it a new car, a new house, a new video game or a new outfit? No matter what it is, something in our souls leaps when we get things. We love it. We have an emotional reaction to new stuff. So it's weird when Solomon tells us there's nothing new under the sun.[18]

But we tend to know these things are shallow, and not ultimately fulfilling.

What about richer, more meaningful pursuits?

Some of us seek to break the cycle by fighting for change through social causes, organizations and charity drives. Others of us look to environmental endeavors or more education as the probable solutions. Sometimes we think the world needs a new political regime or ideology that will usher in more peace.

All of these things can be marvelous.

All of these pursuits can benefit the world.

But Solomon's words challenge our underlying assumptions. Why do you think more education will really fix things in the long run? What lasting effect will more global connectivity or a new political regime really have?

The modern mind relishes in entertaining the idea humanity is on its way upward to endless progress and ultimately utopia. Many enlightenment thinkers pointed to humanity, knowledge, science, and education as solutions that will inevitably lead to heaven on earth. This idea, however, was shaken to its core after the atrocities of World War II and the holocaust. The destruction of the two world wars grew out of technical progress and undermined the basic premise of the Idea of Progress. It remains a matter of debate

---

18 Ecclesiastes 1:9

among intellectuals.[19]

The world is the most educated, most globally connected it has ever been…

And as you read these words, the deadliest war since World War II is raging – *right now* – even though most Americans are unaware of its existence.[20]

We spend $25 billion per year on self-help and counseling…

And the suicide rate has increased 48% from 1950 to 2005.[21]

And so Solomon asks us the question, "Is it working?"

> Do you tend to be pretty optimistic that humanity is on a never-ending upward progress toward utopia? Do you think Solomon is being optimistic, pessimistic, or realistic?
>
> _____
>
> _____
>
> _____
>
> _____

Unfortunately, David Foster Wallace put his hope in education as a primary solution to our interaction with the world's brokenness. He encouraged us that education gives us:

> "The really important kind of freedom… awareness and dis-

---

19 Richard T. Gill (1999). *Posterity Lost: Progress, Ideology, and the Decline of the American Family*. Rowman & Littlefield. pp. 147–48.
20 Tampa, Vava. www.CNN.com. *Why the world is ignoring Congo war.* Nov. 27, 2012. Tampa describes the war as "The same number of lives as having a 9/11 every single day for 360 days, the genocide that struck Rwanda in 1994, the ethnic cleansing that overwhelmed Bosnia in the mid-1990s, the genocide that took place in Darfur, the number of people killed in the great tsunami that struck Asia in 2004, and the number of people who died in Hiroshima and Nagasaki—all combined and then doubled." Over six million people have been killed.
21 **Go to www.midtowncolumbia.com/GoodLifeLinks link #21.** In 1950 the total suicide rate was 7.4 per 100,000 and that number has increased to 11.0 in the last 53 years.

Insight from Ecclesiastes

cipline, and being able truly to care about other people and to sacrifice for them over and over in myriad petty, unsexy ways every day. That is real freedom. That is being educated, and understanding how to think. The alternative is unconsciousness, the default setting, the rat race, the constant gnawing sense of having had, and lost, some infinite thing."

David Foster Wallace recognized we had lost some infinite thing, but he chose to believe an educated mind was the pathway to real freedom. He believed education could deliver to us the good life.

This theory failed him miserably.

Three years after his viral commencement speech at Kenyon College, he committed suicide by hanging himself in November of 2008.

Because education doesn't fix what's wrong with humanity.
Because it's been tried before and it hasn't worked.
And a little more of what already hasn't worked...
... Never works.

"There's nothing new under the sun."[22]

> **Read Romans 8:18-22.** What does it mean that the creation is subjected to futility? How does this passage help us understand Solomon's seeming pessimism?
>
> _____
>
> _____
>
> _____

---

22 For proof of concept in the music industry, check out soundsjustlike.com. The theme of the website was summed up well by Triumph the Insult Comic Dog from the Conan O'Brien show when he said, "I used to like Coldplay so much more, back when they were called U2." **Go to www.midtowncolumbia.com/GoodLifeLinks link #22.**

Read Genesis 3:17-18. Where have you felt like your life is fighting back against you? As if no matter how hard you work for the good life, life just gives you back thorns and thistles?

AWKWARD SILENCE

Deep down in our souls, something tells us Solomon is correct.

But we don't like it.

All of our desperate, vain attempts to break the cycle…

All of our desperate, vain attempts to live the good life…

All of our desperate, vain attempts to get help or to help ourselves…

And deep down we know it's not working.

This is largely why we are so uncomfortable with silence.

Orfield Laboratories in South Minneapolis created a room so quiet it becomes unbearable after a short time. The longest anyone has survived in the 'anechoic chamber' is just 45 minutes.[23]

This might explain why about two-thirds of people aged 30 to 64 frequently watch TV in the hour before bed.[24]

In the TV show, *Dexter*, Dexter's sister Debra explains it as that

---

23 Thornhill, Ted. "We all crave it, but can you stand the silence? The longest anyone can bear Earth's quietest place is 45 minutes" The Daily Mail UK. Link: **www.midtown-columbia.com/GoodLifeLinks link #23.**

24 Dotinga, Randy. "Using Electronics Before Bed May Hamper Sleep" *U.S. News & World Report: Health.* **To read the article, go to www.midtowncolumbia.com/Good-LifeLinks link #24.**

moment "When it gets quiet enough to realize how messed up my thoughts are."[25]

Sitting still and quiet is almost impossible because we start to sense our lives are broken.

Our souls start to show their cracks.

Solomon starts to sound reasonable.

> **Personal challenge:** Turn off all electronics, music, TVs and anything that makes noise you can turn off. Sit in the silence for 5 minutes. What emotions and thoughts did you experience? Make this a game and get a group of people to sit in absolute silence as long as they can until someone cracks from the awkwardness.

_____

_____

_____

_____

GETTING OVER THE SUN

So how do we learn to deal with the cracks in our souls?

How do we learn to handle the silence?

How do we escape the cycle?

How do we deal with the repetitive, boring, meaningless portions of life?

Solomon's answer is there is a sense of meaninglessness in all our work under the sun and we are never going to find a way out of the cycle...

Unless we catch a glimpse of life from beyond the sun.

---

25   *Dexter* is an eight-season SHOWTIME television show that followed the exploits of a vigilante, superhero serial killer. His sister, Debra, is generally not exceptionally deep, but from time to time she nails it in explaining what many of us tend to think and feel.

Unless our work becomes joined to God's forever-enduring work.

> **Read 1 Corinthians 15:58**. Why does Solomon say all of life is vanity but Paul is able to say our work can not be vain? Where have you seen this hold true in your own life?
>
> _____
>
> _____
>
> _____
>
> _____

Paul is echoing Jesus' thought who instructed His disciples, *"Do not work for the food that perishes, but for the food that endures for eternal life, which the Son of man (i.e. Jesus) will give you."*[26] It's the same bell Jesus is ringing when He says not to worry about earthly possessions and pursuits, but to *"seek first God's kingdom…"*

Under the sun, Solomon is right that life is utterly meaningless.

But Jesus didn't come from under the sun.

Jesus enters into the broken cycles of our human existence and offers to us real life.

A real solution.

Jesus comes to give us the good life.[27]

Jesus lets us see life from over the sun.

Jesus offers us a real way out of the cycle. And He offers it to us free of charge. In Jesus, there's hope for our lives to be infused with eternal purpose so we never need ask again, "What's the point?"

He came to get us off the treadmill.

He came to help us see that many people are living and breathing but aren't really alive.

---
26 John 6:27
27 John 10:10

He came to turn our eyes beyond the sun.

But there is a catch.

We don't get to see beyond the sun; we don't get the good life...

Until we join Solomon in the humble admission we are stuck on the treadmill. Solomon is not trying to depress us. He's trying to open our eyes. He is trying to give us eyes to see what is really going on with us. He is offering wisdom and insight that has stood the test of time.

When our perspective is "under the sun," the monotony of life can feel overwhelming. The boring routines of reality can make life feel like a treadmill and then we die. And no matter how hard we try, there is nothing under the sun that helps us break free.

Our only hope is seeing and admitting we're stuck on the treadmill. Then, when we humbly receive Solomon's wisdom, there's a chance our eyes can be opened. There's a chance we can see beyond the sun. Guided by Solomon's wisdom, in Jesus our lives can be joined to God's eternal work and filled with His eternal purpose.

LIFEGROUP DISCUSSION QUESTIONS
CHAPTER 1: THE TREADMILL

1.) Read Ecclesiastes 1:1-11. Where do you see evidence of the treadmill in your life? Where does life feel boring, meaningless, or repetitious? (These could be big, important things, or small, trivial things, or anything in between.)

_____

_____

_____

_____

_____

2.) Where do you see attempts to escape or ignore the boring reality of certain parts of your normal life? (Hobbies, fantasy through books, games or movies, substances, food, relationships, etc.)?

_____

_____

_____

_____

_____

3.) Read Ecclesiastes 1:12-18. Have there been specific moments in your life when God has led you to a despairing agreement with Solomon, that life under the sun is stuck in a cycle? How do these moments help us grow spiritually?

4.) What did Jesus show you in the midst of the "Sit in Silence" personal challenge? Were you able to last for five minutes? How hard was it to turn everything off to create silence in the first place?

5.) How would your life change if you were looking at it from over the sun instead of under the sun? Are there any ways in your life Jesus has helped you turn your eyes beyond the sun? Are there any examples where you see Jesus infusing your life with His eternal purpose?

Pray: Spend some time in prayer together as a group regarding what you've studied. Thank God for anything He's shown you about Himself and the good life. Confess and repent from anything sinful He's shown you about yourself.

I said in my heart, "Come now, I will test you with pleasure; enjoy yourself." But behold, this also was vanity. I said of laughter, "It is mad," and of pleasure, "What use is it?" I searched with my heart how to cheer my body with wine—my heart still guiding me with wisdom—and how to lay hold on folly, till I might see what was good for the children of man to do under heaven during the few days of their life. I made great works. I built houses and planted vineyards for myself. I made myself gardens and parks, and planted in them all kinds of fruit trees. I made myself pools from which to water the forest of growing trees. I bought male and female slaves, and had slaves who were born in my house. I had also great possessions of herds and flocks, more than any who had been before me in Jerusalem. I also gathered for myself silver and gold and the treasure of kings and provinces. I got singers, both men and women, and many concubines, the delight of the sons of man.

So I became great and surpassed all who were before me in Jerusalem. Also my wisdom remained with me. And whatever my eyes desired I did not keep from them. I kept my heart from no pleasure, for my heart found pleasure in all my toil, and this was my reward for all my toil. Then I considered all that my hands had done and the toil I had expended in doing it, and behold, all was vanity and a striving after wind, and there was nothing to be gained under the sun.

So I turned to consider wisdom and madness and folly. For what can the man do who comes after the king? Only what has already been done. Then I saw that there is more gain in wisdom than in folly, as there is more gain in light than in darkness. The wise person has his eyes in his head, but the fool walks in darkness. And yet I perceived that the same event happens to all of them. Then I said in my heart, "What happens to the fool will happen to me also. Why then have I been so very wise?" And I said in my heart that this also is vanity. For of the wise as of the fool there is no enduring remembrance, seeing that in the days to come all will have been long forgotten. How the wise dies just like the fool! So I hated life, because what is done under the sun was grievous to me, for all is vanity and a striving after wind.

Ecclesiastes 2:1-17

CHAPTER TWO
THE EXPERIMENT

WOULDN'T IT BE NICE?
READ ECCLESIASTES 2:1-18

All of us have experienced those moments of envy...

Those moments when we see someone with more than us and we think to ourselves, "Wouldn't it be nice?" Because as we are all chasing the good life, one of the easiest temptations to believe is I just need a little bit *more* to get there. I could really make it happen if I just had more resources.

If I just had a little more money...

If I just had a little more free time...

If I just had a little more intelligence...

If I just had a little more creativity...

If I just had a little bit *more*...

This is why we love movies like Limitless[28], the Brass Teapot[29], and Blank Check[30].

---

28 Limitless was a 2011 production starring Bradley Cooper that explores the effects of a mysterious pill designed to help you access 100 percent of your brain's potential. Cooper's character transforms from a struggling writer to a financial wizard, but he ends up facing many new dangers and troubles and eventually drinks human blood off the floor in a very disturbing scene.
29 The Brass Teapot was a 2012 dark comedy in which a young couple finds a magical brass teapot that will give you money in exchange for your physical pain. The film probes the question, "How much pain would you undergo to get more?"
30 Blank Check is a 1994 classic film in which 12-year old Preston accidentally happens upon a blank check, which he proceeds to make out for *one million* dollars. Hilarity

We love to think about what it would be like if our resource limitations were removed.

This might explain why people buy so many lottery tickets.[31]

> What resource limitations do you believe are prohibiting you from living the good life?
>
> _____
>
> _____
>
> _____
>
> _____

> **Read 1 Kings 4:22-34.** According to this passage what different kinds of resources did Solomon have in excess? Which of these are the most attractive to you? Why?
>
> _____
>
> _____
>
> _____
>
> _____

"I said in my heart, 'Come now, I will test you with pleasure; enjoy yourself.' [...] And whatever my eyes desired I did not keep from them. I kept my heart from no pleasure..."[32]

In Ecclesiastes 2, Solomon sets out on an experiment of epic

---

ensues as Preston uses his million dollars to buy a mansion, a water slide and also tries to avoid getting caught by gangsters who want their money back.
31 U.S. Census data found that over $50 billion was spent on lottery tickets in 2010. **For more information, go to www.midtowncolumbia.com/GoodLifeLinks link #31.**
32 Ecclesiastes 2:1+10.

Insight from Ecclesiastes 39

proportions. With his unlimited money, wisdom, free time, and creativity, he tests all of the pursuits of man to determine if they truly satisfy. What do we mean "all the pursuits"? We mean all of them. Solomon throws off moral restriction and pursues every source of joy humanity regularly indulges in. There's nothing restrained or prudish about his pursuit.

Solomon's experiment puts Charlie Sheen[33], Van Wilder[34], and the Great Gatsby[35] to shame.

Like us, Solomon seeks out entertainment in the form of parties, comedy, and music.

Like us, Solomon pursues pleasure through sexual expression.

Like us, Solomon indulges in rest, relaxation, and comfort.

But unlike us, Solomon has almost no limits on his resources to pursue his experiment. For entertainment, Solomon brings in the best musicians and comedians, the most exciting and dangerous acrobatic acts around. If he performed his experiment in our days, he would have Adele[36], Criss Angel[37], and Cirque Du Soleil[38] all performing in his backyard. That's a heck of a house party to throw

---

33   Charlie Sheen is one of Martin Sheen's two famous sons (along with brother Emilio Estevez). In recent years, Charlie has been infamous for erratic behavior, wild drug use and a crazy party lifestyle.
34   Van Wilder is a fictional character that redefines how epic the college party scene can be.
35   The Great Gatsby is a fictional character created by F. Scott Fitzgerald in his 1925 classic, *The Great Gatsby*. While Gatsby is fictional, Fitzgerald wrote him to be a realistic description of opulence and wild party living in the 1920s.
36   Adele (full name Adele Laurie Blue Adkins) is a British singer-songwriter whose soulful songs have been received with unbelievable success. In total over the past four years, she has been nominated for 179 awards and won 91 of them including an Academy award for best original song in a movie ("Skyfall", 2013), thirteen Billboard awards including "Best artist of the year" in 2012, and nine Grammy awards including seven just for her insanely popular sophomore album, *21*.
37   Criss Angel, self-proclaimed MindFreak, is a young world-renowned magician and illusionist. In 2011, he was awarded the two highest awards in the world of magic: ¹the World Magic Legacy Award recognized him as a Living Legend making Criss the youngest recipient of the award in its history. ²the International Magician's Society welcomed Criss into the Magic Hall of Fame, the organization's highest honor.
38   Cirque du Soleil is a Canadian entertainment company, self-described as a "dramatic mix of circus arts and street entertainment." Cirque du Soleil has produced dozens of shows and won numerous awards including four Primetime Emmys.

for your friends. When Adele needs to rest her pipes, Solomon would bring in Kanye West[39] and Mumford and Sons[40] to play the intermission.

What kind of parties would you throw if you had no limitations on your budget or your connections? What kind of food and drink would you offer? How much would you show off if you could? If you were one of Solomon's guests, he would have brought in James Beard award[41] winning chefs and the fanciest, most exotic food you had ever seen.

Except your plate would be full instead of typical dainty four-star portions.

Solomon kept the bar open always with plenty of reserves.

When the meat for our cookouts starts with *more* than twenty Angus-caliber, grass-fed cows, then we can give Solomon a call and brag to him about our weekend. Commentators agree Solomon's palace hosted fifteen to twenty *thousand* (some estimate thirty to forty thousand) people almost day in and day out for these massive feasts. The largest party we've ever attended looked like an old lady's bridge club compared to Solomon's get-togethers. We are talking about hedonism at its finest.

Unbridled pleasure.

An unlimited open bar.

No end to the delicious juicy meat coming off the grill. Meat wrapped in other delicious juicy meats.

> **Read 1 Kings 11:1-4.** How does the Bible describe Solomon's love life in this passage? Why

---

39 Kanye West is an American hip-hop artist who has won 21 Grammy awards, and over 120 total awards.
40 Mumford + Sons are an English new-folk rock band. In their short career since 2010, they've been nominated for 24 awards and already won 11 awards including a Grammy for Album of the Year in 2013.
41 The James Beard Award is the highest culinary honor a chef can win in America. Recently, Sean Brock, a Charleston chef at the restaurant *Husk*, won the Best Chef Southeast in 2010.

Insight from Ecclesiastes 41

do romantic interests often have an impact on our spiritual health?

_____

_____

_____

_____

When it came to sexual expression, once again, Solomon had no limitations. Over a thousand wives and lovers offered Solomon sexual expression beyond our wildest dreams. No quantity, quality, or frequency of partners escaped Solomon's search for sexual satisfaction. Unbridled free-time and willing partners meant there was no limit to his sexual creativity.

Solomon never thought, "I wonder what that is like?"

He just made it happen.

Read 1 Kings 7:1-12. What do you picture as you read the description of Solomon building his palace? Who comes to mind as modern day empire builders?

_____

_____

_____

_____

Like us, Solomon didn't just settle for shallow pleasures. He added epic empire building to his epic parties.
Like us, Solomon got into gardening...
Except he built forests.[42]

---
42 Ecclesiastes 2:5

Like us, Solomon got into building and decorating...

Except he built mansions for himself and many of his wives.[43]

Like us, Solomon built himself a personal empire to see if the pleasure of accomplishing and building was greater than the pleasure of mindless entertainment.

And when the party was over...

When his impulse to build and accomplish was satisfied...

Solomon sat back and rested while his slaves cleaned up, cooked him meals and took care of all the preparation for the next house party. "*I bought male and female slaves, and had slaves who were born in my house.*"[44]

Solomon's slaves were having slaves.

Solomon had unlimited power, unlimited wealth, and he used these resources to acquire for himself popularity, fun, pleasure, and sex with no seeming end in sight. There's nothing in life Solomon didn't have someone at his beck and call to do for him. He lived the ultimate relaxation. He had no tasks whatsoever to inconvenience him in any way from pursuing pleasure with the full force of all of his time, money, and creativity.

> What would you do with the resources to buy yourself unlimited free time and unbridled pleasure? What kind of good life could you live if you could pay someone else to do every single thing in life you don't enjoy doing?
>
> _____
>
> _____
>
> _____

---

43 Ecclesiastes 2:4
44 Ecclesiastes 2:7

A SNEAK PEEK AT THE END OF THE EXPERIMENT

Read Ecclesiastes 2:11-18. What do you think of Solomon's conclusions at the end of his experiment? Is this what you expected him to say? What in your life would lead you to agree or disagree with his thoughts?

_____

_____

_____

_____

"Behold, all was vanity and a striving after the wind, and there was nothing to be gained under the sun."[45]

In this shocking statement, Solomon is giving us an immeasurable gift.

He's pulling back the curtain on the mystery door and letting us have a sneak peek, pre-released, advanced showing of the end of our pursuits. Solomon gets to the end of his experiment and has time to reflect on all of it. And as he starts thinking, he starts asking questions.

Someone remind me, what's the point of all this?

Why am I throwing this party again?

Are we getting anything from this pleasure?

Are we getting anywhere?

As he started to approach retirement age, Leo Tolstoy, one of the foremost authors of the modern era, started asking the same questions Solomon asks.

---

45 Ecclesiastes 2:11

"My question -- that which at the age of fifty brought me to the verge of suicide -- was the simplest of questions, lying in the soul of every man... a question without an answer to which one cannot live. It was: 'What will come of what I am doing today or tomorrow? What will come of my whole life? Why should I live, why wish for anything, or do anything?' It can also be expressed thus: Is there any meaning in my life that the inevitable death awaiting me does not destroy?"[46]

Put another way, Tolstoy asked himself, "is it all just vanity and striving after the wind?" Does nothing come from the pleasure of the party? Do we gain no lasting purpose from the accomplishment of building an empire? Not a single long term benefit from the relaxation of retirement?

Amazingly, without even thinking about it we all assume if we had unlimited resources to pursue what we desire, then without a doubt, unquestioningly, of course we would be happy. That's what happiness is. Having everything we want. Having unlimited resources to pursue what we want.

But Solomon had everything he wanted.

He had unlimited resources to pursue whatever he wanted.

And somehow his conclusion was it led him to *not* happiness.

How can that be?

Solomon had more money, free time, and creativity to pursue the good life than we will ever have. And in his grace, he's giving us a sneak peek of what we will inevitably conclude at the end of our experiments. He's letting us know our chasing is futile. After chasing anything we could possibly chase to an extent that none of us have the ability to chase it, Solomon's warning is that ultimately, our conclusion—like his—will be that here on earth nothing is lastingly meaningful.

---

[46] Tolstoy, Leo. *A Confession.* www.midtowncolumbia.com/GoodLifeLinks link #46.

At one level, you can read that and say, "Oh, ok. Interesting." But at another level that only reveals your brain is not letting it sink in yet.

This is what all of us think happiness *is*.

The ability to pursue whatever we want... *unhindered*.

And Solomon did it.

Completely wild, free, unbothered pursuit of whatever he wanted.

And he's telling us happiness isn't found there.

> Are there any pursuits in your life where you have started to notice that life never seems to deliver the joy it promises? Have you seen the thrill wear off faster than you expected or fail to match your expectations?
>
> _____
> _____
> _____
> _____

Read Ecclesiastes 2:12-14. Along with having unheard of resources and the benefit of hindsight, Solomon brings one additional source of expertise to the table. Not only did he map out his search of pleasure in a wise and planned out way. He also seeks out foolishness.

Because some people will tell you you can't force the good life.

You just have to let it come to you.

You just have to go with the flow.

Solomon says okay and gives that a try. And even though he concludes it doesn't really matter which approach you take, wise or foolish, pre-planned or free-flow, either way we all still die.

Which one describes you more? Are you more of a free-flow, take life as it comes to you, or are you more of a pre-planned, think through all the options? Are you more type a or type b?

THE THREE COMMON APPROACHES TO LIFE
READ ECCLESIASTES 2:1-10

Maybe even more amazing than the resources of Solomon's experimentation is the vast breadth of his pursuits. As Solomon sets out on his quest for meaning, purpose and the good life, he outlines three distinct stages of life most of us will pass through. These three stages of life provide us with a diagnostic, a sort of grid work to help us see our own lives. In each of the stages, the pursuit of pleasure, accomplishment and relaxation can take different forms.

THREE STAGES OF LIFE:
1. The MTV approach[47]: Youthful Pleasure and Vitality– v. 1-3.
2. The HGTV approach[48]: Adult Accomplishment – v. 4-6.
3. The RLTV approach[49]: Retirement Relaxation – v.7-8.

At the beginning of his journey, Solomon chases the party lifestyle that characterizes a majority of American high school, college and young professional life. In the MTV stage of life, pleasure and excitement take the front seat and accomplishment and relaxation are put on the backburner. "Life of the party" is this approach's nickname. "We can sleep when we die" is the motto. Spring break is its favorite holiday.

---

47 MTV stands for Music Television, a television station launched in 1981 with a target audience of high school students and college students. Although it began as a station to show music videos, most of its content has more to do with shaping young adult life with a specific youthful, partying and vibrant flair.
48 HGTV stands for Home & Garden Television and is a television station that encourages adults in building and improving their homes and gardens by building it themselves.
49 RLTV stands for Retirement living television and is a station that broadcasts travel and leisurely programming specifically targeted towards people in retirement age.

Insight from Ecclesiastes

While the MTV approach typically describes a youthful approach to life, there are certainly plenty of more elderly folks who double dip. In a recent interview with ABC reporter Andrea Canning, Charlie Sheen described his party binge lifestyle as "epic", marked by the finest drugs money can buy and a horde of women he called his "goddesses". But then he said he was clean now and had no worries about relapsing. When Andrea asked him why, he said, "[The drugs] bored the hell out of me after a while."[50]

Solomon would agree.

Is partying and pleasure your primary pursuit?

Are you taking an MTV approach to life?

After attempting the party approach, Solomon moves onto the serious business of life, building things and accomplishing goals and earning awards. He starts this stage with the summary, "I made great works." From houses, to vineyards to gardens, parks and forests, Solomon literally built a small empire. The palace he built for himself took twice as long to build as the time it took to build the temple in Jerusalem. He also built homes for many of his three *hundred* wives.

Donald Trump is the spokesperson for the HGTV approach to life. Business leadership is the only type of literature they recognize and no holidays are celebrated while embracing this approach. "We can sleep when we die" is still the motto but for a totally different reason. In its worst form, this second approach to life turns into full on workaholism where family, friends, and social life are traded in for eighty-hour workweeks, big promotions, and even bigger accolades. But even in smaller forms, there's an odd sensation the first time you decide of your own volition you want to go outside and work in your yard. You actually choose to do that which felt like punishment for most of your adolescence. Because it feels good. Building things feels good. Contributing feels mature and awe-

---

50 For more, go to www.midtowncolumbia.com/GoodLifeLinks link #50.

some.

A HGTV approach to life typically describes adulthood although some adolescents begin building and accomplishing at an early age and some elderly never desire to stop building. If you take this approach, pleasure and relaxation take a backseat to the sheer adrenaline rush of accomplishing.

Or better put, the pleasure of accomplishing trumps every other form of pleasure.

Is building an empire your primary pursuit in life?

Are you taking a HGTV approach to life?

After demolishing the HGTV approach to life, Solomon adopts a third and final approach to life: retirement. Reflection. Relaxation. He moves from working his tail off all day long, to sitting on his tail all day long. In his old age he looks at all the wealth he's gathered and mobilizes it like little soldiers to go fight for and maximize the comfort of his La-Z-Boy. He brings some of the singers back from his partying days, but this time it's easy listening with Neil Diamond, Celine Dion, and the Eagles[51].

In the RLTV approach to life, accomplishment and raw pleasure typically take a backseat to comfort and relaxation. Travel, family, shopping, and leisure activities often fill up many retirees lives as they try to make the most of their last days on earth.

While most people wait until retirement to take a RLTV approach, some actually approach most of life from this vantage point. For some, pure pleasure and accomplishment are never that enticing and they take a relaxed approach from day one.

Are you approaching life from a kicked back La-Z-Boy, or RLTV approach?

Though the different stages overlap and inter-

---

[51] Neil Diamond, Celine Dion and the Eagles are all incredibly recognized artists from the 1960s to the 1990s. Put together they have won over 160 major awards and been nominated for more than 300.

weave, which of the three common stages of life do you currently resonate with most?

_____

_____

_____

_____

And despite the fact that Solomon had unheard of resources to pursue the good life...

And despite the fact that Solomon pursued both pre-planned and free-flow pleasure...

And despite the breadth of his search eclipsing the three most common life stages...

He still says inevitably we will find all of these pursuits are meaningless under the sun.

LEARNING FROM THE EPIC EXPERIMENT

As hard as Solomon's experiment and conclusions are for our minds to grasp...

The grasping is where all the benefit is.

If it's true the wisest and one of the richest, most powerful men who ever lived...

If he really did set out to pursue happiness in any and every way he could imagine...

And if he really did his experiment with unbridled resources...

And if he really did throw off moral restrictions...

If he did exactly what all of us wish we could do...

And if he really did conclude that all of it is meaningless...

Then we have to at least ask the question, right?

What if all the things I'm chasing after really aren't going to satisfy me?

In a recent interview, Pastor Matt Chandler commented on this uncertain foundation of the pursuit of happiness in our culture:

> "If you're paying attention, our culture is ripe with examples of why our culture's way isn't working... Hey, this is what culture's telling you is going to make you happy, is going to fulfill your life, is going to make you satisfied, and yet, has that happened? Aren't you all pursuing that? Isn't this what you've been trying? Hasn't this led to heartache? Hasn't this led to disappointment? Aren't you still in your heart of hearts being nagged by something? 'How's that working for you? Maybe God's way would be a better way'... I have yet to run across legitimate statistics that support that if you just do whatever feels right to you, you're going to live a fulfilled, happy, glad life. I mean, that's not working."[52]

The rich and the famous give us ample examples of what Chandler is referring to. In an article with Rolling Stone, Brad Pitt comments,

> "The emphasis now is on success and personal gain. I'm sitting in it, and I'm telling you, that's not it. I'm the guy who's got everything. I know. But I'm telling you, once you get everything, then you're just left with yourself. I've said it before and I'll say it again: It doesn't help you sleep any better, and you don't wake up any better because of it. Now, no one's going to want to hear that. I understand it. I'm sorry I'm the guy who's got to say it. But I'm telling you."[53]

---

[52] **To read the entire interview, go to www.midtowncolumbia.com/GoodLifeLinks link #52.**

[53] Brad Pitt interview with Chris Heath. "The Unbearable Bradness of Being". *Rolling Stone*. October 28, 1999. **To read the article, go to www.midtowncolumbia.com/**

Jim Carrey adds to Pitt's comments:

"I hope everybody could get rich and famous and will have everything they ever dreamed of, so they will know that it's not the answer."

But at the end of the day, Pitt and Carrey are just telling us what we already know in the deepest places in our souls. These celebrities aren't the authority on our lives, we are. And have we not yet seen that we chase after exactly what culture tells us to chase after? Have we not yet seen that the things we chase tend to leave us empty eventually?

Why do we continue to believe just a little *more* would change something?

Solomon is graciously telling us it won't.

> *"And still he seeks the fellowship of his people and sends them both sorrows and joys in order to detach their love from the things of this world and attach them to himself."*

> *- J.I. Packer*

GoodLifeLinks link #53.

LIFEGROUP DISCUSSION QUESTIONS
WEEK 2: THE EXPERIMENT

1.) Read Ecclesiastes 2:1-8. If you had almost unlimited resources of time, money and energy and could experiment like Solomon did, what would your experiment look like? Use your imagination. What would you do? Where would you go? Where would you look first in your quest for the good life?

_____
_____
_____
_____
_____

2.) Is there any part of you that believes if you just had a little bit more _____ (opportunity, money, pleasure, comfort, accomplishment) then you would really be satisfied? Does Solomon's experiment have any impact on your thoughts on these cravings?

_____
_____
_____
_____
_____

3.) Think about the three common stages of life. What stages have you been through so far? Though the different stages overlap and interweave, what stage best describes your life currently?

_____

_____

_____

_____

_____

4.) Read Psalm 73. How is Jesus helping detach your hands and your love from the things of this world and attaching them to Himself?

_____

_____

_____

_____

_____

Pray: Spend some time in prayer together as a group regarding what you've studied. Thank God for anything He's shown you about Himself and the good life. Confess and repent from any ways you're chasing experimental sources of satisfaction instead of finding it in Jesus.

I hated all my toil, in which I toil under the sun, seeing that I must leave it to the man who will come after me, and who knows whether he will be wise or a fool? Yet he will be master of all for which I toiled and used my wisdom under the sun. This also is vanity. So I turned about and gave my heart up to despair over all the toil of my labors under the sun, because sometimes a person who has toiled with wisdom and knowledge and skill must leave everything to be enjoyed by someone who did not toil for it. This also is vanity and a great evil. What has a man from all the toil and striving of heart with which he toils beneath the sun? For all his days are full of sorrow, and his work is a vexation. Even in the night his heart does not rest. This also is vanity.

There is nothing better for a person than that he should eat and drink and find enjoyment in his toil. This also, I saw, is from the hand of God, for apart from him who can eat or who can have enjoyment? For to the one who pleases him God has given wisdom and knowledge and joy, but to the sinner he has given the business of gathering and collecting, only to give to one who pleases God. This also is vanity and a striving after wind.

Ecclesiastes 2:18-26

CHAPTER THREE
THE TROPHY CASE

THE TROPHY CASE
READ ECCLESIASTES 2:18-23

Depression and suicide rates skyrocket when people retire.

Does that strike you as counterintuitive?

Isn't retirement supposed to be a happy place?

A land of milk and honey and golf and relaxation?

But the numbers don't lie. According to a 2013 report by the Institute of Economic Affairs, "Retirement increases the probability of suffering from clinical depression by about 40 percent."[54] The National Institute for Mental Health found that "Older Americans are disproportionately likely to die by suicide." Americans over the age of sixty-five commit suicide 27% more frequently than the average.[55]

Author Skye Jethani records an exercise one of his supervisors used to help him understand this surprising trend when he was training to be a hospital chaplain:

> "On a series of note cards [my supervisor asked me to] write down things that gave my life meaning: relationships, activ-

---
54 For more, go to www.midtowncolumbia.com/GoodLifeLinks link #54.
55 For more, go to www.midtowncolumbia.com/GoodLifeLinks link #55.

ities, accomplishments, work, memories, etc. The thirty cards were laid out on the table in front of me as my supervisor began telling the imaginary story of my aging. First my body began to weaken. Cards with activities I enjoyed were removed. Eventually my work disappeared. Vital relationships were lost; my wife died. As the story continued fewer cards remained, even joyful memories faded away as my mind weakened. With just a few note cards left, my supervisor asked, 'How would you feel if this was all that remained of your life?' 'Lost', I replied. 'I would feel lost. There's nothing left. I would have no purpose.'"

Personal Challenge: Take twenty index cards or small sheets of paper and write the twenty most valued projects, people and pursuits in your life right now. Imagine how your life will play out over the years and how and when the cards will disappear or be taken from you. What thoughts and feelings do you notice throughout this exercise?

_____

_____

_____

_____

Have you ever thought about the fact that something is hardwired in all of us to do and accomplish things? Despite the thrill of entertainment and relaxation, there is something in us that chooses to build, make, and achieve. Even much of our entertainment (including video games, musical instruments, and sports) involves competition, a mission we are trying to complete or a task we are trying to master.

Trophies tell us we accomplished something important.

They tell us we did something significant.

They tell us we matter.

We refer to trophy fish[56], trophy scars[57], and even trophy wives[58]. Each in a way refers to having accomplished something.

In America, work is the engine of the dream.

We have the ability to work, and therefore the ability to climb the ladder and make something of ourselves. We have the ability to achieve and build empires for ourselves, no matter what our background. In some way, this is why we pay attention to the lives of the rich and the famous. We see them as shining examples of what we hope to be able to accomplish.

This is why Americans have historically been known for working incredibly hard…

And hating work at the same time.

According to the International Labour Organization, "Americans work 137 more hours per year than Japanese workers, 260 more hours per year than British workers, and 499 more hours per year than French workers."[59]

At thirteen days, Americans take the least vacation time annually of countries in the industrialized world. The British take 28 days. Brazilians get 34. Italians come in at 42.

Dr. Timothy Keller explains Genesis' unique explanation for where our desire to work and accomplish things comes from.

"The Bible begins talking about work as soon as it begins

---

56 A trophy fish is a caught fish that is so impressive as to be one worthy of winning a trophy if it had been caught in a competition.
57 A trophy scar is a scar that comes with an impressive story of some accomplishment or rare feat.
58 A trophy wife is a term that refers to a very attractive wife that a husband wants to show off because of her good looks.
59 Miller, G.E. *20 Something Finance.* "The U.S. is the Most Overworked Developed Nation in the World – When do we Draw the Line?" **To read the article, go to www.midtowncolumbia.com/GoodLifeLinks link #59.**

talking about anything – that is how important and basic it is. The author of the book of Genesis describes God's creation of the world as work. In fact, he depicts the magnificent project of cosmos invention within a regular workweek of seven days. And then he shows us human beings working in paradise. This view of work – connected with divine, orderly creation, and human purpose – is distinct [to the Genesis creation narrative] among the great faiths and belief systems of the world..."[60]

Unlike most faiths, Genesis sees creation as the achievement and beautiful success of God's work and not the result of some war or conflict between spiritual beings.

"In the beginning, [...] God worked. Work was not a necessary evil that came into the picture later, or something human beings were created to do but that was beneath the great God himself. No, God worked for the sheer joy of it."[61]

Have you ever thought about Keller's point that God seems to enjoy work (doing, building, and accomplishing)? Does that have any effect on how you think about accomplishing in your life? If so, what effect?

_____

_____

_____

_____

---

60 Keller, Timothy. *Every Good Endeavor* (New York, NY: Penguin Group, 2012) p. 33.
61 Ibid, p. 34-35.

Read Genesis 2:15 and Deuteronomy 8:17-18.
What are the implications of God asking Adam to build, cultivate, and work before the fall in Genesis? Have you ever thought about the fact God designed us to accomplish things?

_____

_____

_____

_____

Unfortunately, the Genesis narrative of God's beautiful design for accomplishing and doing comes to a bitter and untimely end. Like sweat's impact on the underarm of a white t-shirt, sin leaves a filthy and irreversible mark on all of our pursuits. This yellowed stain is the vanity of toil Solomon observes throughout Ecclesiastes.

But note that in this passage, Solomon isn't just talking about our jobs. He's talking about everything we do: from building a family, to parenting children, to pursuing relationships, or working on our careers and our hobbies and our homes and our communities. And his conclusion is that all of it is vain toil. Solomon is presenting us with the reality check that there is no endeavor in our lives that has not been kissed by the curse of the fall.

STILL HAVEN'T FOUND WHAT WE'RE LOOKING FOR

To help us understand why our toil is vain, Solomon points us to a deep problem inherent to the human accomplishment project. Ever since the Genesis fall, we humans have been looking to our doing to give us a sense of identity. This is commonly seen in the American culture of asking, "What do you do?" as a first question when we meet someone.

When you hear the word teacher, lawyer, or engineer, do specific types of people come to mind?

That is because in our culture, teacher, lawyer, and engineer are more than professions.

They are identities.

This specifically career-based sense of performancism is part of why depression and suicide rates rapidly increase when people retire.

We believe we are what we do.

So if what we do is taken away…

Then we cease to know who we are.

We feel lost.

We feel hopeless.

We are ill prepared to face the meaninglessness of life without work and tasks to undertake.

> How much do you understand your identity in light of your projects (work related or other)? If you lost the ability to work, what range of emotions would you undergo?
>
> _____
>
> _____
>
> _____
>
> _____

When the world moved from the Genesis design to the Genesis fall, work became toil. The fall affects much more than our employment. It's impact runs much deeper than surface-level frustration and annoyance (though it causes that too). Toil means work and accomplishment are a place where we try to find our identity instead of finding it in Jesus. Toil means accomplishment is a source of security and insecurity instead of resting our security in Jesus. (Job security is more than good standing with your boss.) Toil means some of us tend to seek approval through our work. "Hey! Look at this. Did you notice all these impressive things I've done?" Bosses and co-workers often provide a primary source of adult peer pressure and social anxiety.

In all of these toil symptoms, we are asking what we do to be something it was never intended to be. Our productivity cannot provide the deepest longings of our soul because it was never designed to do so in the first place. We are asking a toilet to cook us toast. It's not equipped for the task.

We are human beings.

Not human doings.

That's a somewhat cheesy way to say it. But it gets the point across.

Solomon laments, "*What has a man from all the toil and striving of heart with which he toils beneath the sun? For all his days are full of sorrow, and his work is a vexation. Even in the night his heart does not rest.*"[62] Our hearts are full of sorrow because our work is unable to answer our deepest questions. Our hearts can't rest because we still haven't found what we're looking for.

A dozen plaques on the wall and still it's not enough.

A hundred promotions…

A thousand pats on the back…

And still we hunger for more.

Because we never catch a big enough trophy fish to make ourselves matter.

Our trophy cases are never impressive enough to give us a lasting identity.

Simply, we are not what we do.

Our value is not the sum of our successes, nor is it the sum of our failures.

Your accomplishments will never answer the deepest questions of your soul. Who am I? Why am I here? What's the point? Am I significant? Am I a somebody? You will find the answer to none of these questions printed on the back of your paycheck. The people you work so hard to impress can never put your heart's concerns at ease.

> Where do you notice yourself believing what you do or accomplish defines you and gives you value?
>
> _____
> _____
> _____
>
> What would you say if I asked you, "Why do you matter? What makes you significant? What do you bring to the table?" Would your answers tend to be things you can do or attributes of who you are?
>
> _____
> _____
> _____

WE CANNOT CONTROL WHAT HAPPENS TO THE FRUIT OF OUR LABOR

Along with the deep understanding our accomplishments cannot satisfy the deep questions of our soul, Solomon is also haunted by a logistical question:

"What if the kid who inherits all my stuff is an idiot?"[63]

Recently, a handful of the rich and the famous have responded to Solomon's question by deciding their children won't inherit their fortune. Jackie Chan is one such celebrity, who recently changed his will so one hundred percent of his $130 million estate will be donated to charities instead of his only son, Jaycee (not to be confused with Jay-Z[64]). Chan is quoted as explaining, "If he is capable, he can make his own money. If he is not, then he will just be wasting my money." Gina Rinehart, who was recently named the richest woman in the world, said her kids "lacked the requisite capacity or skill, knowledge, experience, judgment, or responsible work ethic [to manage the business and family inheritance.]"[65]

Sharing Chan and Rinehart's point of view, "Warren Buffett, Bill Gates, and Ebay founder Pierre Omidyar are some of the more notable billionaires who have pledged their entire fortunes to charity. Buffett is an especially staunch opponent of what he calls "dynastic wealth" (wealth so vast it creates generational dynasties). Buffett refers to anyone who grew up wealthy as a 'member of the lucky sperm club' and, like Jackie Chan, firmly believes if his children work hard enough they can achieve great success the same way he did."[66]

> Do you agree or disagree with these celebrities? If you built a fortune, how much of it would you give

---

[63] Ecclesiastes 2:18-19. For more information about what actually happens to Solomon's inheritance, read 1 Kings 11:42-43 and 2 Chronicles 12:1-16. After Solomon's death, his son Rehoboam reigns, but the kingdom is shattered, split in two and Rehoboam's reign is a constant war. Solomon's fears seem fairly substantiated as Rehoboam's reign is a large contrast to Solomon's forty years of peace.

[64] Jay-Z is a prolific rapper and hip hop artist. He is in no direct way related to Jackie or Jaycee Chan.

[65] Frank, Robert. "Millionaire Parents Say Their Kids Are Unfit to Inherit" **To read the article, go to www.midtowncolumbia.com/GoodLifeLinks link #65.**

[66] Warner, Brian. "Jackie Chan's Son Will Get None Of His $130 Million Fortune" **To read the article, go to www.midtowncolumbia.com/GoodLifeLinks link #66.**

to your children as an inheritance (None of it, some percentage, or all of it)?

_____

_____

_____

And while these celebrities share some of Solomon's perspective, he would actually push the question even further asking, "How do I know the charity won't end up run by some fool who still ends up wasting my fortune?" His simple point is humans cannot build a truly lasting empire. While we can certainly have some impact on those who come after us, most of us don't know even the first names of our great-great grandparents. Douglas O'Donell makes this point by testing our memory on hugely influential historical figures, "Can you name any of the rulers of the Aztec Empire?... Can you name five pre-1960s vice presidents of the United States?"[67]

Julius Caesar's Rome is gone.

So is Alexander the Great's Greece.

So is Attila the Hun's nomadic empire.

Even if people remember any of your accomplishments, will they care about them? A group of our pastors was discussing this question and one of them recalled looking at his father's high school trophy case. His father was featured in the case multiple times. Oddly the pastor observed, "If anyone on planet earth would care about that trophy case, it should have been me, his son. But I really wasn't all that interested."

At some point in overvaluing our accomplishments and our achievements, we become like Uncle Rico in Napoleon Dynamite,

---

67 O'Donnell, Douglas. *The Beginning and End of Wisdom* (Wheaton, IL: Crossway, 2011) p. 67.

consumed with the past.[68] To make this clarifying, personal, and a bit unsettling, think about this:

> What are you giving your life to that will matter two hundred years from now? How about one hundred years from now? Even fifty short years from now?

_____

_____

_____

_____

GRACE AND MISSION – WORKING WITH GOD
READ ECCLESIASTES 2:24-26

There are three distinct ways Jesus redeems the doing of our lives: 1. Everything in our lives is a gift of grace. 2. Work is just work. 3. Jesus invites us to join Him in His eternal purpose and mission. From Solomon's seat on the bus, he points us to all three of them by encouraging us to view work from above the sun.

1. Everything in our lives is a gift of grace.

"There is nothing better for a person than that he should eat and drink and find enjoyment in his toil. This also, I saw, is from the hand of God, for apart from him who can eat or who can have enjoyment?"[69]

---

[68] Napoleon Dynamite is a 2004 coming of age story about an awkward high school student named Napoleon who really enjoys tater tots. His Uncle Rico relishes in the past often specifically boasting about his ability to throw a football. At one point, he claims to be able to throw a football over a distant mountain range. His obsession with his past accomplishments makes him appear to be a fool.
[69] Ecclesiastes 2:24-25

Despite his general refrain that all toil is vanity and striving after the wind, here Solomon pauses to recognize that work and the enjoyment of accomplishing are gifts that come *"from the hand of God."* Paul adds to this perspective in his letter to the church in Colossae:

> *"Whatever you do, work heartily, as for the Lord and not for men, knowing that from the Lord you will receive the inheritance as your reward. You are serving the Lord Christ."*

If God was actually your boss at work – if God was the one dictating your every pursuit in life – what would the office vibe feel like? What would your personal and family vibe be like? Would you be stressed all the time? Would you be slaving away trying not to make God mad? Or would you be bored and doing the bare minimum to not get noticed?

I don't think so.

"Work heartily... knowing that from the Lord you will receive inheritance as your reward." As Christians, the very center of our lives is Jesus' grace. Because of the cross, we have been adopted into God's family and we are now treated as His kids.[70] We have an inheritance coming that would blow our minds if we could understand it.

So Paul says, work hard with Jesus' grace in mind.

Work hard never forgetting the undeserved inheritance you've got coming.

In God's office, when a co-worker is having a terrible day, everyone pauses just long enough to make her feel completely loved, but not so long productivity is affected. Every failure is a coaching moment. Every success is motivation to work even harder.

In Jesus, there's a way to see our toil from a vantage point beyond the sun.

There's a way to see all of our doing as a gift of grace.

---

70 Romans 8:15, Galatians 4:4-7, Ephesians 1:5

Every opportunity to build, every project, every job is actually a gift from God our Father. This understanding immediately infuses God into our view of our labor no matter how difficult it might be. Every hardship is a way Jesus is stretching and growing my character.[71] Every skill, desire, and opportunity (and really my entire life) is nothing more than a gift of grace. Moses reminds the Israelites of this accomplishment-as-grace perspective in Deuteronomy:[72]

> How do you see your skills, your jobs, and your opportunities as gifts from God?

_____

_____

_____

_____

2. Work is just work.
When we view work from over the sun, in light of the gospel, we no longer need to look to our accomplishments to try to answer our deepest questions. Who are you? Why are you here? Are you significant? Are you a somebody? All of these questions are answered fully in the gospel.

In a heartbreaking interview with Vogue, Madonna revealed her inability to see accomplishment from above the sun:

> "My drive in life comes from a fear of being mediocre. That is always pushing me. I push past one spell of it and discover myself as a special human being but then I feel I am still mediocre and uninteresting unless I do something else. Because even though I have become somebody, I still have to prove

---

71 Hebrews 12:7-11
72 Deuteronomy 8:18

that I am somebody. My struggle has never ended and I guess it never will."[73]

The need to achieve Madonna talks about is unfortunately common in our hearts. But in Jesus, there is a way out from this performance driven cycle. In Jesus, you are God's child, rescued by Jesus' blood[74]. You are here because a loving God created you with His own hands for His glory and your joy.[75] The point of life is knowing God and resting in His perfect love for you.[76] You are significant because Jesus paid His precious blood to purchase you and chooses to make you significant.[77] In Jesus, you aren't just a somebody. You are the beloved child of God almighty.[78]

The more we see life from above the sun…

The more we rest in these spiritual realities of the gospel…

The more we will see we don't need our accomplishments, promotions, or trophies to try to gain a sense of identity.

We already have one.

> How are you actively resting in your gospel identity? Have you seen any ways God's grace in Jesus has reshaped how you view work, accomplishments and doing?
>
> _____
>
> _____
>
> _____
>
> _____

---

[73] Madonna quoted from an article in Vanity Fair, April 1991. **To read the article, go to www.midtowncolumbia.com/GoodLifeLinks link #73.**
[74] Ephesians 1:3-7
[75] Psalm 139:13-16
[76] Matthew 22:37 and John 6:28-29.
[77] Luke 15:4-6 and 1 Corinthians 6:19-20
[78] 1 John 3:1

And when work is just work, now I'm free to use my work to love other people instead of trying to use my work to impress people. Success is optional. Pastor and author Tullian Tchividjian explains this freedom in his book, *Jesus + Nothing = Everything*:

> "Because Jesus was extraordinary, you're free to be ordinary. Because Jesus succeeded for you, you're free to fail. Because Jesus won for you, you're free to lose."

3. Jesus invites us into His eternal purpose and mission.

From above the sun, we can now view all projects, work and accomplishment as a vocation, not just work.[79] A job is a vocation only if someone else calls you to do it and you do it for them, rather than for yourself. Martin Luther explained:

> "Your work is a very sacred matter. God delights in it, and through it he wants to bestow his blessing on you. This praise of work should be inscribed on all tools, on the forehead and faces that sweat from toiling."

All accomplishing is meaningful when Jesus is our boss.
When we work for Him…
When we work with Him in mind…
When we work with a view of His grace as the only reason we have the ability to achieve anything, our work is filled with joy and meaning. Solomon recognizes this reality that all of our wealth – the fruit of all our accomplishing – is a gift from God that can be only be truly enjoyed when it is received as a gift of His grace. But he also warns us this perspective is lost when we become hyper-focused on life under the sun.

---

[79] This sentence assumes that the project you are considering is not directly sinful, harmful or oppressive to others.

"For apart from him who can eat or who can have enjoyment?"[80]

Apart from God's grace, none of us actually have the ability to toil for anything in life. And apart from God's grace, none of us can experience the deep enjoyment of viewing our labor as a gift of God's grace.

> List all of the ways God's grace has opened up the opportunities you have to seek different pursuits, careers and accomplishments.
>
> _____
>
> _____
>
> _____
>
> _____

"I believe that ambition – godly ambition, that is – is a noble force for the glory of God… The Bible teaches that people are created by God to desire – and to go after those desires with single-minded determination. It's this capacity to desire and strive that can generate remarkable good or stupefying evil… God uses small people to steer the course of history."[81]

Dave Harvey's book, *Rescuing Ambition*, outlines what happens when our ambition to achieve and accomplish in life is taken hostage by a vision of the glory of God. Harvey continues:

"While our ambitious impulses lead us to vain pursuits, the Lord of glory has come to rescue our ambition. He has come to redeem us and recapture us for His glory…Ambition be-

---

80 Ecclesiastes 2:25
81 Harvey, Dave. *Rescuing Ambition* (Wheaton, IL: Crossway, 2010) p. 14.

gins with knowing who we are in Christ and what we're give because of that fact. But it trains itself... according to the agenda God sets for us. He shapes our ambition for the role He wants us to play in His plan."[82]

As much as the grace of God reshapes our perspective, attitude, and motive for accomplishing, the mission of God reshapes the direction of our accomplishing. The truth is Jesus calls us not only to work for Him as our boss; not only to work motivated by His grace and His inheritance, but also to work *with* Him, joining Him in His mission of rescuing and restoring the lost. Solomon touches on this in chapter 3:

> *"I perceived that whatever God does endures forever; nothing can be added to it, nor anything taken from it. God has done it, so that people fear before him. That which is, already has been; that which is to be, already has been; and God seeks what has been driven away."*

Instead of wasting our lives building temporary kingdoms that won't last once we're gone, Jesus invites us to join Him and build His eternal kingdom. I love how Solomon describes God's work in v. 15:

> *"God seeks what has been driven away."*

Since the curse, all of human effort has been driven away from God's eternal purpose. But God seeks us. He chases and pursues and desires to restore us to His beautiful eternal kingdom and design.

God seeks what has been driven away.

And He invites us to join Him in seeking what has been driven away.

---

82 Ibid, p. 32 and 70.

> *"And he said to them, 'Follow me, and I will make you fishers of men.'"*[83]

> *"Through Christ, [God] reconciled us to himself and gave us the ministry of reconciliation;"*[84]

> *"And he made from one man every nation of mankind to live on all the face of the earth, having determined allotted periods and the boundaries of their dwelling place, that they should seek God, and perhaps feel their way toward him and find him."*[85]

When we allow Jesus' grace to motivate our every endeavor – when we begin to see the ways Jesus has shaped and placed our lives to join in His mission – we can escape the meaningless toil of life under the sun. We no longer need to believe our work validates us. We are free to live out of Jesus' validation. We have a new purpose of seeing as many as possible come to know the eternal validation that only comes as a gift of Jesus' grace.

---

[83] Matthew 4:19
[84] 2 Corinthians 5:18
[85] Acts 17:26-27

LIFEGROUP DISCUSSION QUESTIONS
WEEK 3: THE TROPHY CLUB

1.) Read Ecclesiastes 2:18-26. Solomon explains that all of our toil under the sun is vanity and striving after the wind. Where in your life have you felt work, goals, and accomplishments feel utterly pointless?

_____

_____

_____

_____

_____

2.) Where are you most tempted to believe your accomplishments define your identity?

_____

_____

_____

_____

_____

Fill in the blank: It would crush my soul if I suddenly lost the ability to _____ .

3.) Read Ephesians 2:1-10. The gospel says our identity is perfectly, fully, and eternally defined by Jesus' work for us in the cross.

Where are you asking your accomplishing to give to you identity that is already yours in Jesus?

_____
_____
_____
_____
_____

4.) What steps do you need to take to begin to view your tasks as gifts of Jesus grace? In what ways does God want to use your abilities and your ambition for His glory and mission? Are there any pursuits in your life that, if you are honest, are driven by a need for validation, or ability to feel good about yourself, and need to be somebody? How can your group encourage and help you in this area?

_____
_____
_____
_____
_____

Pray: Spend some time in prayer together as a group regarding what you've studied. Thank God for anything He's shown you about Himself and the good life. Confess to your group where you are tempted to find your identity in your personal trophy case. Pray for each other to repent and walk motivated by Jesus' grace and toward Jesus' mission.

For everything there is a season, and a time for every matter under heaven: a time to be born, and a time to die; a time to plant, and a time to pluck up what is planted; a time to kill, and a time to heal; a time to break down, and a time to build up; a time to weep, and a time to laugh; a time to mourn, and a time to dance; a time to cast away stones, and a time to gather stones together; a time to embrace, and a time to refrain from embracing; a time to seek, and a time to lose; a time to keep, and a time to cast away; a time to tear, and a time to sew; a time to keep silence, and a time to speak; a time to love, and a time to hate; a time for war, and a time for peace.

 What gain has the worker from his toil? I have seen the business that God has given to the children of man to be busy with. He has made everything beautiful in its time. Also, he has put eternity into man's heart, yet so that he cannot find out what God has done from the beginning to the end. I perceived that there is nothing better for them than to be joyful and to do good as long as they live; also that everyone should eat and drink and take pleasure in all his toil—this is God's gift to man.

 I perceived that whatever God does endures forever; nothing can be added to it, nor anything taken from it. God has done it, so that people fear before him. That which is, already has been; that which is to be, already has been; and God seeks what has been driven away.

Ecclesiastes 3:1-15

CHAPTER FOUR
THE ILLUSION OF CONTROL

THE INGREDIENTS
READ ECCLESIASTES 3:1-8

This passage is one of the most famous passages in all of scripture due to its regular appearances in pop culture. In 1965, the Byrds turned this text into a hit single.[86] In 1989, it provided the title for Grisham's bestselling novel, *A Time to Kill*.[87] "A time to be born, and a time to die"[88] has been quoted at 99% of all funerals ever.[89] CSI and True Blood both tilted episodes, "Turn! Turn! Turn!"[90] Fahrenheit 451 ends with "To everything there is a season, and a time

---

86 The Byrds are a band from California formed that in 1964. Though they didn't maintain the long lasting success of contemporaries like the Beatles, the Beach Boys, and the Rolling Stones, critics today consider the Byrds as one of the most influential bands of the 1960s. Many see them as the innovators of folk rock combining rock influences from the British Invasion bands (the Beatles + the Monkees) with more traditional American folk music. Ironically, their two biggest hits were both covers, as *"Turn, Turn, Turn"* was originally written by Pete Seeger and *"Mr. Tambourine Man"* was penned by Bob Dylan.
87 *A Time to Kill* was John Grisham's first novel and initially only sold about 5000 copies. After his second, third and fourth novels (*The Firm*, *The Pelican Brief* and *The Client*)
88 Ecclesiastes 3:2
89 This is a science fact.
90 CSI and True Blood are both popular television shows on CBS and HBO respectively. CSI stands for Crime Scene Investigation and follows detectives and investigators trying to understand confusing crimes. True Blood is a vampire drama.

for every matter under heaven."[91] But despite its consistent cultural presence, most of us haven't truly meditated on the deeply insightful and perplexing nature of this list.

Much of our modern existence is designed to convince us we are in control.

Thermostats allow us to control the precise temperature of our environments.

Safety equipment minimizes the negative impact of a slip, fall, or spill.

Medications attempt to help us manage our depression, our anxiety, and even our appetite.[92]

Smart phones let us control our bank accounts, our schedules, and our social networks anywhere we have a signal.

And all of these technological advancements and gadgets perpetuate the idea we are in control. Unfortunately, that conclusion is an illusion. Solomon's poem at the beginning of Ecclesiastes chapter 3 sounds nice when we first read it. There's a time for every season of life. Well, isn't that nice?

But the brutal reality is Solomon is telling us that all of the seasons of life come, and when they come, how they come, and why they come are well beyond our ability to control.

> When in your life have you noticed you were completely unable to control the season of life you were experiencing? What thoughts and emotions did you experience as a result?

---

[91] Fahrenheit 451 is a dystopian novel by Ray Bradbury in which books have been outlawed and firemen set houses on fire if books are found in them.

[92] A wide variety of anti-depressants are used to help people manage symptoms of depression including Prozac, Celexa, Zoloft and Wellbutrin. To control anxiety, some doctors recommend tranquilizers and benzodiazepines including Xanax, Valium, and Klonopin. To control appetite, appetite-suppressants like phentermine and Belviq are frequently prescribed.

In our modern comfortable American existence, there is something inside of us that is almost offended by the reality of the universe Solomon is helping us to see in this poem. We inherently believe without question we are able to control our quest for the good life.

And Solomon's poem quietly and firmly responds— No. You're not.

Solomon is doing much more than describing the seasons of human life. He is communicating to us where these seasons come from and therefore the reality we are unable to control them. William Brown writes:

> "Even though humanity is the grammatical subject of the various infinitives – people plant and pluck up, mourn and dance – the human subject is by no means the determiner of such events. [The passage] makes clear that God alone is the one who determines; God is the primary, albeit implicit, actor on the temporal scene. The ever-constant swings of time's pendulum are suspended and held firmly by God."[93]

> Why is it hard to think of God being in control of all the seasons of life? What questions does this idea bring to your mind?

---

93 Brown, William P. *Ecclesiastes* (Lousiville, KY: John Knox, 2000) p. 42

Read Isaiah 46:8-11. According to this passage, what is unique about God compared to anyone else in all of creation? How is God's perspective different from ours? What are the implications of God being able to see everything in all of history all at the same time?

Read Psalm 115:3 and 135:6. Does this idea of God being able to do whatever He wants make you uncomfortable? Why or why not?

The Scriptures repetitively introduce God as being unique, powerful, and in control like no one else in the universe.[94] Many times, God introduces Himself and explains, "Let's get one thing straight.

---

[94] Exodus 8:10, Deuteronomy 4:35+39, 6:4, 2 Samuel 7:22, 22:32, 1 Kings 8:60, 2 Kings 19:15, 1 Chronicles 17:20, 1 Chronicles 29:11-12, Nehemiah 9:6, Job 42:2, Psalm 18:31, 103:19, Isaiah 37:20, Mark 12:29, John 5:44, Romans 16:27, 1 Corinthians 8:4, 1 Timothy 1:17

No one else is like I am.[95] I alone sit on top of time. I alone sit above all of human history and view it all at the same time. From the beginning to the end, everything is under my gaze. I set it to motion. I'm the one who decides. A hawk doesn't go chasing after a mouse without me saying, 'Fetch.'" At the end of his life, King Nebuchadnezzar is graciously restored from his pride-driven insanity and he echoes the Psalms:

> "His dominion is an eternal dominion; his kingdom endures from generation to generation. All the peoples of the earth are regarded as nothing. He does as he pleases with the powers of heaven and the peoples of the earth. No one can hold back his hand or say to him: 'What have you done?'"

This simple but profound explanation of God's supremacy makes us uncomfortable because it reveals to us the eternal reality that we are not in control. And this returns us to our problem with the poem in Ecclesiastes chapter 3. The seasons mentioned in the poem are not pick-and-choose items. They are realities of life that come for us whether we want them to or not. They are inevitabilities.

THE WHINY MIDDLE SCHOOLER IN ALL OF US

Being told we are not in control doesn't land very well with most of us.

Part of that is because we tend to be fairly well off Americans.

People who live in war torn, politically unstable, or impoverished areas rarely believe themselves to be in control. When you don't know whether or not you will eat tomorrow, or whether or not you might be shot in the street, the illusion of control doesn't carry much weight.

Another part of the illusion is we tend to not think much on

---

95 Deuteronomy 32:39, Isaiah 43; 10, 44:6-8, 45:5+18+21, 46:9

the reality that one phone call, one conversation, or one letter can change everything. Before you finish reading this chapter any of us could receive life-altering news.

And that scares us.

Because somewhere deep down we subconsciously believe we are in control.

So we try to dismiss anything that shows us the contrary as quickly as possible.

> Have you ever had a phone call, letter, or conversation that brought large unexpected change in your life (positive or negative) that was beyond your control?
>
> _____
> _____
> _____
> _____
>
> **Read Matthew 6:25-27.** Jesus' simple point is that worry and anxiety reveal our illusion of control. No matter how hard we try, we cannot add a single hour to our life. What are areas of our lives over which we do have some control? What are areas of our lives in which we have no control?
>
> _____
> _____
> _____
> _____

What I don't tend to think about very much is the reality that people who never experience pain often turn out to be self-centered, spoiled-rotten, and vicious people. The more the circumstances of my life allow me to believe I really am in control, the more entitled and self-absorbed I tend to end up.

But this isn't just theoretical to us. Each of us, in different ways and to differing extents, has dealt with pain, suffering, and sorrow. And the thought that *my* pain, *my* suffering, and *my* sorrow somehow passed through God's hands before entering *my* world strikes a strange chord in *me*.

What are we supposed to do with this?

At some level that question will never be answered. Pastor Matt Chandler comments:

> "You will never know it all because mystery is a prerequisite of faith and trust. The soul needs it. We can't function without there being question marks as badly as we want those question marks to be periods."

Solomon explains this same idea in v. 11 when he says, *"[God] has put eternity in man's heart, yet so that he cannot find out what God has done from the beginning to the end."* God has set a desire to see the big picture in our hearts, but He's done it in such a way we are never able to comprehend it fully. So part of the answer is a humble acceptance of the fact we will never fully understand the whole big picture.

But another part of the answer is resting in the fact God is the one painting the big picture and He is unbelievably trustworthy. God is baking a dish that involves many ingredients, and whether or not we enjoy each and every individual ingredient, God promises that the end result will be amazing.[96]

See, no one likes eating flour.

---

[96] Romans 8:26-28

But almost everyone likes eating cake.[97]
And we can't have cake without flour.

> Can you think of times in your life where God used your pain to grow you? Have there been moments in your life where everything was confusing, frustrating, or painful until you were able to see God's beauty and purpose in hindsight?

_____

_____

_____

_____

CONTROLLING OUR RELATIONSHIPS

One of the foundational books that many counselors rely on for personal counseling is a book called Boundaries by Henry Cloud. A technique and one of the central images the book uses to help people understand healthy boundaries is to imagine a mental hula-hoop lying on the ground around your feet. Everything inside that hula hoop – namely you – is your responsibility. Everything outside that hula-hoop is outside of your control and therefore you are not responsible for it.

One of the hardest places for people to apply this idea is in the context of relationships. I am not in control of what other people think of me or how they respond to me. I'm not responsible for their thoughts about me. So much social anxiety and depression boils down to attempting to manage and control other people's imagined thoughts about us.

---

[97] If you do not enjoy eating cake, please contact Brandon Clements, our pastor who oversees care, counseling and Recovery ministries. His email is bclements@midtown-columbia.com

Do you see any examples of internal anxiety because you are concerned about what other people think about you? Have you ever considered the reality you cannot ultimately control what they think?

_____

_____

_____

_____

Read 1 Peter 5:5-6. How does acknowledging God's mighty hand lead you to let go of your anxiety?

_____

_____

_____

_____

Consistently the Bible encourages us not to try to control other people. A parent who tries to control their children in an unhealthy manner is warned to be careful not to embitter their children.[98] A wife who tries to hard to control her husband is described as a nagging form of torture.[99] At the end of the day, the Bible encourages us to take responsibility for what God has placed inside our hula-hoop and to relinquish the desire to control other people.

CONTROLLING OUR SPIRITUAL GROWTH AND HEALING

---

98 Colossians 3:21
99 Proverbs 19:13 and 27:15

"Evidently some people try to control even the processes of healing by 'understanding them...' Paul Stern, a psychiatrist at Harvard University, said twenty-five years ago that the most difficult defense to overcome in therapy is 'intellectualization,' that is, attempting to control therapy by analyzing our problems and articulating the reasons for them."[100]

Quoting Paul Stern, J. Keith Miller points us to our control issues that often times show through even in our quest for spiritual growth and healing. Allowing Jesus to grow and heal us slowly is a process that requires patience. Patience is not something that comes naturally to many of us. So, we try to control the process by over thinking it and forcing it to happen on our timetable.

For many of us, this controlling instinct even affects our relationship with Jesus as we try to control our spiritual growth through strictly regimented spiritual disciplines. We can become obsessed with our own spiritual growth. We start to look like a child who wants his parents to keep measuring his height on the doorframe to see if he's grown in the past five minutes. One of our pastors described this as a farmer who keeps pulling his crops out of the ground to see if their roots are growing.

> **Read Mark 4:26-29.** What does growth look like in the kingdom? Where have you seen this kind of slow growth where you put in effort and have to wait to see the results?
>
> _____
>
> _____
>
> _____

---

100   Miller, J. Keith. *A Hunger for Healing* (New York, NY: Harper Collins Publishers, 1991) p. 47.

ACCEPTING OUR LACK OF CONTROL

The good news is coming to see God's control over the seasons and ingredients of our lives frees us up to receive every moment of our lives as a gift. The bad news is living in light of this reality is dang near impossible and in some ways it encapsulates the entire difficulty of life as a Jesus-follower.

The process for how we grow in accepting a lack of control is summed up in the simple word: *surrender*.

Pastor and author John Ortberg explains this connection:

> "The reality of this world is that I was born into Someone Else's kingdom. My life came to me as a gift I did not choose; it is suspended from a slender thread that I did not weave and cannot on my own sustain. 'Many are the plans in a human heart, but it is the Lord's purpose that prevails.' So I will need to... surrender. I crown another to be Master – Lord – of my life. I offer my gifts, energies, resources, and heart to Him."[101]

The humility of realizing we are not in control leads us to take a spiritual posture of surrender. For Christians, this is not a one-time moment when we become a Christian. This is the ongoing process of growth where we climb down off the throne of our lives over and over. We continually surrender our self-righteous desire to handle life on our own and to reject assistance. We continually allow Jesus' grace to grow our faith.

Unfortunately, the continual process of surrendering control is extremely difficult. I do not naturally or gladly surrender my will, my desires, and my control. In *A Hunger for Healing*, J. Keith Miller applies the twelve-step program from Alcoholics Anonymous to the Christian life. Commenting on the third step, he writes:

---

[101] Ortberg, John. *When the Game is Over, it All Goes Back in the Box* (Grand Rapids, MI: Zondervan, 2007) p. 63.

"This idea of surrendering, of releasing authority and control of outcomes to another, is a very difficult notion for thinking persons. Not only does surrendering go against all our childhood injunctions to 'do it yourself' and 'don't give up,' but as long as we can keep our minds churning, we can keep from facing and understanding our own part in causing our painful feelings. Another stumbling block for Christians [is that] many Christians live their lives as if God is their servant and [exists to] help them attain their goals." [102]

> Do you ever see this temptation in your own life? Where are times you have tried to control God or tried to treat him like your servant? Do you ever get mad at God if he doesn't answer yes to your prayers right away?
>
> _____
>
> _____
>
> _____
>
> _____

In The Reason for God, Dr. Timothy Keller picks up on this idea of seeing God as a subservient being we can control.

> "If you don't trust God enough to let Him challenge and correct your thinking, how could you ever have a personal relationship with God? In any truly personal relationship, the other person has to be able to contradict you.

---

[102] Miller, J. Keith. *A Hunger for Healing* (New York, NY: Harper Collins Publishers, 1991) p. 47-48.

For example, if a wife is not allowed to contradict her husband, they won't have an intimate relationship. Remember the movie The Stepford Wives? The husbands of Stepford, Connecticut, decide to have their wives turned into robots who never cross their wills. A Stepford wife was wonderfully compliant and beautiful, but no one would describe such a marriage as intimate or personal.

Now, what happens if you eliminate anything from the Bible that offends your sensibility and crosses your will? If you pick and choose what you want to believe and reject the rest... you'll have a Stepford God! A God, essentially, of your own making, and not a God with whom you can have a relationship and genuine interaction."[103]

The real danger in refusing to surrender control to God is we lose out on the possibility of a real relationship with Him. To construct a Stepford God we can control cuts off any possibility of the single thing we were most designed for— relationship with Jesus. Solomon concludes,

"I perceived that there is nothing better for them than to be joyful and to do good as long as they live; also that everyone should eat and drink and take pleasure in all his toil – this is God's gift to man."

A life lived in surrender to God's goodness, in full view of the reality I am not in control, is an incredible gift from God. We are freed up to view the seasons of life as gracious ingredients from a loving God who is trustworthy no matter how bad the seasons

---

[103] Keller, Timothy. *The Reason for God* (New York, NY: Penguin Group, 2008) p. 117-118.

may feel. When I cease attempting to control God, I find joy in the reality of knowing Him as He is, without any figments of my imagination trying to paint Him in one convenient color or another.

The beauty of letting go is you get to live in reality.

The beauty of surrender is you become truly free.

The beauty of giving up control is you get real relationship with God.

> What areas of your life are you struggling to surrender to God's control?
>
> _____
> _____
> _____
> _____
>
> In what ways have you constructed a Stepford God you are trying to control, instead of surrendering to and loving God for who He is? How vibrant is your relationship with God? Are you eager to spend time with Him, talk to Him, and learn from Him?
>
> _____
> _____
> _____
> _____

LIFEGROUP DISCUSSION QUESTIONS
WEEK 4: THE ILLUSION OF CONTROL

1.) Read Ecclesiastes 3:1-8. As you thought through this poem during the personal story, what were some of the most defining moments that stand out in your life? Are there any seasons in this poem you recognize in your defining moments?

_____
_____
_____
_____
_____
_____

Looking back are you able to see how God has orchestrated—or allowed— these moments and seasons for your good and His glory?

_____
_____
_____
_____
_____
_____

2.) Where do you struggle with the concept of faith, trust, and mystery? Are there any pains in your life that have planted deep seeds of mistrust towards God?

_____
_____

_____
_____
_____
_____

3.) Read Ecclesiastes 3:9-13 and Luke 12:22-34. What does surrendering control to Jesus look like on a daily basis in your life? Are there any areas in your life that are particularly difficult to surrender?

_____
_____
_____
_____
_____
_____

How does surrender to God's control relate to anxiety and contentment?

_____
_____
_____
_____
_____

4.) How comfortable would you be telling God He can do whatever He wants with your life? How fully can you tell God you trust him to give you what he knows you need, not what you think you need? Would you tell God you would do whatever He asked of you, no matter what? If not, what do you think prevents you from praying such a prayer?

_____

_____

_____

_____

_____

_____

Pray: Spend some time in prayer together as a group regarding what you've studied. Thank God for anything He's shown you about Himself and the good life. Confess to your group where you are tempted to try to control your life and struggle with surrendering control.

Again I saw all the oppressions that are done under the sun. And behold, the tears of the oppressed, and they had no one to comfort them! On the side of their oppressors there was power, and there was no one to comfort them. And I thought the dead who are already dead more fortunate than the living who are still alive. But better than both is he who has not yet been and has not seen the evil deeds that are done under the sun.

Then I saw that all toil and all skill in work come from a man's envy of his neighbor. This also is vanity and a striving after wind.

The fool folds his hands and eats his own flesh.

Better is a handful of quietness than two hands full of toil and a striving after wind.

Again, I saw vanity under the sun: one person who has no other, either son or brother, yet there is no end to all his toil, and his eyes are never satisfied with riches, so that he never asks, "For whom am I toiling and depriving myself of pleasure?" This also is vanity and an unhappy business.

Two are better than one, because they have a good reward for their toil. For if they fall one will lift up his fellow. But woe to him who is alone when he falls and has not another to lift him up! Again, if two lie together, they keep warm, but how can one keep warm alone? And though a man might prevail against one who is alone, two will withstand him—a threefold cord is not quickly broken.

Better was a poor and wise youth than an old and foolish king who no longer knew how to take advice. For he went from prison to the throne, though in his own kingdom he had been born poor. I saw all the living who move about under the sun, along with that youth who was to stand in the king's place. There was no end of all the people, all of whom he led. Yet those who come later will not rejoice in him. Surely this also is vanity and a striving after wind.

Ecclesiastes 4:1-16

CHAPTER FIVE
FLYIN' SOLO

FLYIN' SOLO
READ ECCLESIASTES 4:9-11

Irene Taviss Thomson in her book, Culture Wars and Enduring American Dilemmas, describes individualism as "the quintessential American value." In other words, according to Thomson, there is nothing more truly and deeply American than independence.

Our largest patriotic holiday is called Independence Day.[104]

The greatest movie ever made has the same title.[105]

We tell each other to be your own person.

Express yourself.

Pull yourself up by your bootstraps.

Don't let anyone infringe on your pursuit of happiness.

I am master of my fate:

I am the captain of my soul.[106]

---

[104] American Independence Day is celebrated on the 4th of July, commemorating our independence from Great Britain. It is best celebrated by floating down the river, preferably while wearing jorts, red-white-and-blue colored anything, and something with an eagle if possible. Also, fireworks are a necessity.

[105] *Independence Day* is a 1996 American science-fiction movie and won the Academy Award for Best Visual Effects and grossed over $800 million. The claim that it is the greatest movie ever is highly debated by scholars. However, everyone on planet earth agrees that it is Will Smith's best movie.

[106] These lines come from the poem *Invictus*, written by British poet William Ernest Henley, and published in 1875. This poem has been quoted in no less than a dozen American art forms, making appearances from classics like *Cassablanca* to more contem-

Independence is a general characteristic of being able to handle life on your own without needing to rely on assistance or support from others. On July 4th, in the year 1776, America emphatically declared that we did not need Great Britain's assistance in governing ourselves. We could do it by ourselves.

This same attitude appears in many of our mentalities toward relationships and our lives. I can do it by myself. I do not need anyone's assistance. I'm a grown man. This sense of relational independence and isolation results from personality wirings as well as our responses to life experience (i.e. those who have been burned in relationships are often less trusting in current relationships.).

> Would you say you are more independent or more dependent on social relationships? Thinking through your life, what drives and motivates your independence?
>
> _____
>
> _____
>
> _____

The statistics agree with Thomson's assertion. According to a General Social Survey conducted by the National Science Foundation in 2006 and printed in the American Sociological Review:

- If family members are not counted, over half of Americans have no one outside their immediate family with whom they can share confidences.
- The number of "socially isolated" Americans has doubled since 1985.

porary works like *30 Rock*.

- The number of people who indicated they had a neighbor with whom they could confide has dropped more than half since 1985— from around 19 percent to about 8 percent.
- Compared with 1985, nearly 50 percent more people in 2004 reported their spouse is the only person they can confide in.
- According to the 2006 census, one-fourth of the nation's households — 27.2 million — consisted of just one person, compared to 10 percent in 1950. That's a 250% increase.

Where does this isolation come from? It's rooted in our love of individualism. This kind of individualism says my personal hopes, dreams, pursuits, and preferences are of more significance than the good of the community I belong to. When relationships are difficult or there is friction, I simply withdraw and seek out others with whom I can have more comfortable interactions. Very few people in our society put down roots in a particular place with a particular group of people and stick it out through good times and bad. All the while, we bemoan the loneliness we feel due to the shallowness of our relationships.

> Do you see any evidence of this isolation in your own life? What about in your co-workers, neighbors, and family members' lives? How do you think this social isolation is connected to the American value of independence?
>
> _____
>
> _____
>
> _____
>
> _____

In the fourth chapter of Ecclesiastes, Solomon turns his attention to consider social isolation, independence, and the human need for community. This theme shows up at the beginning when Solomon considers the oppression and abuse in the world in v. 1:

> *"And behold, the tears of the oppressed, and they had no one to comfort them! On the side of their oppressors there was power, and there was no one to comfort them."*[107]

Observing oppression and the abuse of power, Solomon laments the pain of isolation for the downtrodden. For any of you who have been through hard times, you know how much more painful those times can be when there is no one to comfort you. He picks back up on this same idea in v. 9:

> *"Two are better than one, because they have a good reward for their toil. For if they fall, one will lift up his fellow. But woe to him who is alone when he falls and has not another to lift him up! Again, if two lie together, they keep warm, but how can one keep warm alone? And though a man might prevail against one who is alone, two will withstand him—a threefold cord is not quickly broken."*[108]

Solomon speaks with the clarity and wisdom of experience as he reveals to us the dangers of individualism. Three times Solomon paints the warmth and profit of a shared communal life and the corresponding detriment of a separated life. Two have a good reward for their toil because they help each other up when one falls down. Two lying down together can keep warm[109]. Two (or three) can stand against an attack from an enemy.

But what happens if we fall down and no one is there to help? What happens if we're trapped in the winter seasons of life with

---
107 Ecclesiastes 4:1
108 Ecclesiastes 4:9-12
109 To be clear, he's talking hypothermia prevention, not baby making

no one to keep us warm?

What happens if a bully attacks us when we are all alone?

In a fallen world, as fallible humans, there are going to be days when we trip, slip, and fall. If we isolate ourselves, those days can be detrimental instead of minor setbacks.

> Can you think of times in your life where you have gone through hard times alone? What about hard times where people were there to support you? What were the differences in the two types of experiences?
>
> _____
>
> _____
>
> _____
>
> _____

A wealth of contemporary scientific research is actively confirming Solomon's ancient wisdom. When dealing with stressful situations, a robust social support network helps to reduce psychological distress such as anxiety or depression.[110] Social support also helps significantly if you are dealing with chronic high stress due to rheumatoid arthritis, cancer, stroke, or coronary artery disease. Conversely, low social support is hugely detrimental. People who are more isolated demonstrate higher rates of major mental disorder than those with high support. These include post-traumatic stress disorder, panic disorder, social phobia, major depressive disorder, and eating disorders.[111]

Every major pastoral counseling issue we face as a church and in

---

110 Taylor, S.E. "Social support: A Review". In M.S. Friedman. *The Handbook of Health Psychology*. (New York, NY: Oxford University Press, 2011). pp. 189–214.
111 If you would like to study more into the scientific research regarding the negative impacts of individualism, and the positive impacts of social support **go to www.midtowncolumbia.com/GoodLifeLinks link #111.**

our LifeGroups is benefited (in both symptom-reduction as well as life quality and longevity) by community involvement. Every major issue we face is damaged by individualism.

> The three largest decisions we make in our culture are who we marry, where we live, and what career(s) we pursue. We absolutely stress out over each of these, and experience an unparalleled amount of anxiety in our lives compared to most cultures before us. Much of this is because in those cultures, people made these decisions together with their community around them, allowing those closest to them to give input and even to have "veto" privileges. This sort of vulnerability makes us incredibly uncomfortable.

Despite all of the scientific research and all of the real life pastoral experience I've seen, there is something in me that wrestles with what Solomon is saying here. We are red, white, and blue-blooded Americans after all. Individualism is part of what makes us great.

We like our space.

We like our me-time.

Despite any amount of clinical based research to corroborate Biblical wisdom, part of me kind of wishes the Bible didn't say this. I know Jesus says the world will know we love Him by the way we love each other, but for a number of reasons (fear, laziness, selfishness) there are parts of me that still prefer isolation, self-protection, and a lone ranger mentality. Elyse Fitzpatrick picks up on this hesitance:

> "[This] kind of fellowship flies right in the face of our American individualism and desire for privacy. We don't want anyone poking around in our affairs, and we certainly don't want to be accused of poking about in anyone else's. This idolatry

of privacy and individualism is one of the greatest detriments to sanctification in the church today. God has placed us in a family because we don't grow very well on our own... The kind of biblical relationship to which I think the New Testament calls us is almost nonexistent."[112]

> What parts of your life are marked by individualism, isolation, and privacy? What parts of your life are marked by openness, fellowship, and community?
>
> _____
>
> _____
>
> _____
>
> _____
>
> What hesitancies, fears, anxieties, or resistances do you have to the idea of living a shared life in gospel community?
>
> _____
>
> _____
>
> _____
>
> _____

FIVE PITFALLS THAT DAMAGE GOD'S COMMUNITY
READ ECCLESIASTES 4:1-16

In Jesus, God invites us to see His family and His design for com-

---

[112] Fitzpatrick, Elyse. "The Idolatry of Individualism", *The Resurgence*. **To read the article, go to www.midtowncolumbia.com/GoodLifeLinks link #112.**

munity from over the sun. He invites us to agree with Him and the wealth of medical research that indicates the solo life isn't good for us. But there are things that keep us from accepting God's gracious invitation. Surrounding his warning about individualism and his commending of a shared community life, Solomon observes five personal toxins that destroy communal life: jealousy, laziness, discontent, overwork, and pride. Each attack us internally and magnetically pull us away from the becoming the type of community God envisions for us.

JEALOUSY

> *"I saw that all toil and all skill in work come from a man's envy of his neighbor. This also is vanity and a striving after wind."*

Solomon notes that envy of our neighbors separates people instead of drawing them together. When we constantly treat our lives like a comparative competition, constantly trying to one up each other, we are unable to serve and love our neighbor because we are always trying to climb over him to the top. Paul warns of this human competitive drive in Galatians, *"But if you bite and devour one another, watch out that you are not consumed by one another."*

The word picture is a pack of wild dogs so hungry they would devour each other.

Jealousy makes us act like a pack of wild animals.

Jealousy makes us lash out in malicious gossip and harsh unfair critiques of others.

Jealousy steals our ability to rejoice in other's successes.

Jealousy causes us to celebrate a tiny bit when others fail.

Have you seen this in your life? In your LifeGroup?

And at an even deeper spiritual level, jealousy reveals we aren't resting in the fullness of love and identity Jesus gives us freely. Pastor and author Tullian Tchividjian explains:

"Christians who are no longer sure that God loves and accepts them in Jesus, apart from their present spiritual achievements, are subconsciously insecure persons... envy, jealousy, and other branches on the tree of sin grow out of their fundamental insecurity."[113]

> Where have you seen jealousy negatively impact your ability to walk in healthy, vibrant community? Where have you seen the gospel set you free from jealousy in real practical ways?
>
> _____
>
> _____
>
> _____
>
> _____

LAZINESS

"The fool folds his hands and eats his own flesh."[114]

Solomon's description sounds almost identical to his picture of laziness in the sixth chapter of Proverbs:

"Go to the ant, O sluggard; consider her ways, and be wise... How long will you lie there, O sluggard? When will you arise from your sleep? A little sleep, a little slumber, a little folding of the hands to rest, and poverty will come upon you like a robber, and want like an armed man."[115]

---

113 Tchividjian, Tullian. "Insecurity Produces Pride". *The Gospel Coalition Blog*. **To read the article, go to www.midtowncolumbia.com/GoodLifeLinks link #113.**
114 Ecclesiastes 4:5
115 Proverbs 6:6 and 9-11

This passage addresses laziness' impacts on economic stability but it also applies to our pursuit of community. Is Solomon saying it's foolish to rest well? Of course not. The picture Solomon paints of laziness is choosing that which is easy over that which is healthy for you.

Your laziness chooses ease over health.

When we choose to watch TV instead of hanging out with our LifeGroup...

When we choose to seek our own pleasure instead of serving others...

When we choose to sit passively and not engage in good conversation...

We are picking something easy over something good.

Solomon explains that in doing so we eat our own flesh. We harm ourselves. This happens all the time in our pursuit of gospel community.

"What do you mean? I make an effort! I try to make friends."

I have no doubt you do. I have felt this same frustration. But the reality of sin makes communal living hard, awkward, and broken at times. So, the question is not "did we try?" The question is, "have we worked hard, prayed hard and loved hard until Jesus forms His beautiful community out of sinful humans like us?"

Lazy community always chooses the friends I have over welcoming in new friends.

Lazy community chooses to bail rather than to fight hard in prayer.

Lazy community demands others love me well and never asks the question, "Am I loving anyone the way I want to be loved?"

Intimacy requires work. Gospel community requires effort and wrestling.

Read Galatians 6:7-10 and Hebrews 12:1-3.
Are there any ways laziness is impacting your pursuit and perspective of community? How does the gospel motivate you to not grow weary of doing good?

_____

_____

_____

_____

DISCONTENT

"Better is a handful of quietness than two hands full of toil and a striving after wind."[116]

One of the loudest, most annoying, most damaging landmines that destroys gospel community is when we turn into loudmouthed complainers. Instead of love, we bring two hands full of toil to our relationships. Instead of grace, we brings a self-righteousness that exudes, "If everyone would just be as awesome as I am, then this group would be great."

When we are discontent, we never consider if we are part of the problem. We just point the finger at all the problems, but never bring any viable solutions. And we certainly don't work to bring those solutions to life.

Discontentment tricks us.

It makes us think our role in community is to critique it.

Instead of humbly believing Jesus has placed us in community to help love it and to help build it. A massive theme of the gospel is Jesus chose to love us when we were not very lovable. Romans 5:8 expresses it this way: *"God shows his love for us in that while we*

---
[116] Ecclesiastes 4:6

were still sinners, Christ died for us." Jesus had plenty to complain about and be discontent with us when He chose instead to love us and welcome us into His family. He didn't pick us because of what we brought to the table. He didn't welcome us because we were lovely. He chose to love us in such a way that He makes us lovely over time.

> Do you spend more time complaining about the weaknesses of your community, or working to help your community grow? How in the past month have you responded to frustrations with your community by prayer and service instead of grumbling and division?

_____

_____

_____

_____

BUSYNESS

> *"Again, I saw vanity under the sun: one person who has no other, either son or brother, yet there is no end to all his toil, and his eyes are never satisfied with riches, so that he never asks, 'For whom am I toiling and depriving myself of pleasure?' This also is vanity and an unhappy business."*[117]

Discontent, laziness, and jealousy are slightly easier to spot in ourselves because they are at least a specifically negative thought and attitude. Busyness is sneakier. Busyness happens when we fail to correctly prioritize our time and energy toward the most important things. Our lives become consumed with urgent tasks and

---
[117] Ecclesiastes 4:7-8

Insight from Ecclesiastes

issues that are often not bad at all.

They are fine.

Sometimes they are even good.

They always feel urgent.

And they can absolutely rob us from the most important things in life.

This can often happen with work as in Solomon's example. Pastor and author John Ortberg retells the parable of the rich young man who Jesus called a fool because he wanted to build bigger barns instead of being rich towards God. Ortberg speculates about his overwork and its effect on his family and community:

> "And though he was a very bright guy, he… said to himself when he felt guilty, 'I'm doing it all for them.' Of course this was not even partly true. He would have lived this way if they didn't exist at all. He lived this way even though they begged him to change. [He continued to say to himself] 'I'm doing it all for them.' And no one knew him or loved him enough to tell him the truth."[118]

See how tempting this is? I'm working for them! Sixty, seventy, even eighty or more hours a week. And I end up never really seeing those I say I'm working for. Even in the short times I am present, I end up disengaged, exhausted, and distracted. When we are overworked and failing to see our family, it is highly unlikely we are going to make time for our LifeGroup.

> What would your spouse, your children and your LifeGroup say about the health of your work habits?

---

118 Ortberg, John. *When the Game is Over, it All Goes Back in the Box* (Grand Rapids, MI: Zondervan, 2007) p. 22.

But busyness is not limited to work. In a sinful broken world, there will always be plenty of excuses to not hang out with people and build deep relationships. Our schedules get rapidly filled with an onslaught of children's activities, housework and cleaning that renders us unable to give the time and energy that deep relationships require.

We end up looking a lot like Martha.[119]

And Solomon warns us once again: It's vain. It's meaningless.

If we don't wake up, we're going to die lonely and it won't be until our deathbed we realize we over busied ourselves to death. Oftentimes, busyness is kissing cousins with laziness.

So after busying ourselves all week…

Laziness chooses ease over health…

And watching TV is always easier than hanging out with people.

Especially when we've had such a busy, busy day.

It never dawns on us everyone else might be busy too. And they are less without us. And we are less without them.

And the busyness will never end.

So at some point we're going to have to prioritize the importance and beauty of deep relationships.

> What good things get in the way of you prioritizing the time and energy it really takes to build deep,

---

[119] In Luke 10:38-42, Jesus stops by Mary and Martha's house where Martha is so busy (doing good things like serving people) that she misses out on the most important thing of hanging out with Jesus. We do this same thing with carving out time to spend with Jesus and also with carving out healthy time to spend building deep, healthy relationships with church family.

lasting healthy relationships in biblical community?

_____

_____

_____

_____

PRIDE

> *"Better was a poor and wise youth than an old and foolish king who no longer knew how to take advice."*

At the root of all sin and specifically the sin that unravels the beautiful community Jesus is building in us is pride.

Pride fuels jealousy that says, "I deserve what others have!"

Pride fuels laziness that says, "I deserve a break!"

Pride fuels discontent that says, "I deserve for people to listen to my complaints!"

Pride fuels busyness that says, "What I am doing is very important!"

Solomon, and Jesus, loves us enough to say, "Wake up. Because a day is coming when you are going to fall. A winter season is coming when you are going to be freezing cold in your isolation. An attack is coming you can't anticipate and you won't be able to handle alone."

So let's humble ourselves and press into Jesus. Let's let Him expose our pride and our jealousy and our laziness and our discontent and our overwork. Let's let Him heal us and let Him enfold us into His community.

> Are there any places in your heart that believe you can handle life better on your own than in community? Do you tend to believe that other people get

in your way, mess up your plans and just complicate life?

_____

_____

_____

_____

How can you humbly accept and enjoy the beautiful design Jesus has built you for community?

_____

_____

_____

_____

LIFEGROUP DISCUSSION QUESTIONS
WEEK 5: FLYIN' SOLO

1.) Do you tend to be more of an independent person or more socially connected? Why? As a group, speak into what you see as the tendencies in each other.

2.) Read Ecclesiastes 4:9-11. As you studied you were asked to think through the story of your life and specifically about times when you have fallen down, gone through winter seasons, or faced surprise attacks. Were you well prepared and surrounded by community or were you isolated, lonely, and cold? How can your community help you be more prepared for these times in the future?

3.) Which of the five toxins Solomon warns us about in this passage do you struggle with the most? Why?

4.) Read Romans 12:12. This verse occurs in a passage where Paul is describing how to live as gospel-centered community and it provides the antidote to the toxins Solomon warns us about in Ecclesiastes 4.

How does Jesus actually provide you with whatever you are looking for in your jealousy, laziness, discontent, overwork, or pride?

How can you repent as a group and grow in being joyful in hope, patient in affliction, and faithful in prayer?

5.) If we fully understood the community Jesus created us for and fully repented from the dangers Solomon warns us about, what would that beautiful community look like?

Pray. Spend some time in prayer together as a group regarding what you've studied. Thank God for anything He's shown you about Himself and the good life. Confess to your group where you are tempted to run to individualism and repent by encouraging each other to trust Jesus and let Him grow us in selfless love.

If you see in a province the oppression of the poor and the violation of justice and righteousness, do not be amazed at the matter, for the high official is watched by a higher, and there are yet higher ones over them. But this is gain for a land in every way: a king committed to cultivated fields.

He who loves money will not be satisfied with money, nor he who loves wealth with his income; this also is vanity. When goods increase, they increase who eat them, and what advantage has their owner but to see them with his eyes? Sweet is the sleep of a laborer, whether he eats little or much, but the full stomach of the rich will not let him sleep. There is a grievous evil that I have seen under the sun: riches were kept by their owner to his hurt, and those riches were lost in a bad venture. And he is father of a son, but he has nothing in his hand. As he came from his mother's womb he shall go again, naked as he came, and shall take nothing for his toil that he may carry away in his hand. This also is a grievous evil: just as he came, so shall he go, and what gain is there to him who toils for the wind? Moreover, all his days he eats in darkness in much vexation and sickness and anger.

Behold, what I have seen to be good and fitting is to eat and drink and find enjoyment in all the toil with which one toils under the sun the few days of his life that God has given him, for this is his lot. Everyone also to whom God has given wealth and possessions and power to enjoy them, and to accept his lot and rejoice in his toil—this is the gift of God. For he will not much remember the days of his life because God keeps him occupied with joy in his heart.

Ecclesiastes 5:8-20

CHAPTER SIX
THE CHAMPAGNE CLUB

JUST A LITTLE BIT MORE
READ ECCLESIASTES 5:8-12

Why do we care so much about celebrities? Have you ever thought about that? From tabloids to style magazines, magazines.com lists twenty-five different celebrity oriented magazines circulating in the US.[120] Just these magazines – which do not make up an exhaustive list – circulate more than 20 million copies every year. Even if you don't personally care about the rich and the famous, as a culture we are obsessed with them.

From athletes to actors to politicians and musicians…
From magazines to websites to television shows…
We love observing those with more than us.
We give the rich and the famous a louder voice in our culture. Without really even thinking about it, we generally assume that what they think and say matters. We inherently believe they are worth listening to and paying attention to.

Why do you think that is?

At least part of the reason is because they have more stuff than we do. If you are honest with yourself, you have to admit celebrities have some very cool stuff.

For more, go to www.midtowncolumbia.com/GoodLifeLinks link #120.

Jerry Seinfeld had a bowling alley built into his mansion.[121]
Johnny Depp owns his own island in the Bahamas.[122]
Kanye West and Kim Kardashian own a private helicopter.[123]

Tom Cruise has a collection of airplanes including a P-51 Mustang and a Gulfstream IV that reportedly cost over $28 million and is outfitted with a Jacuzzi and a screening room for watching movies.[124]

Stuff is fun. In some ways, we all like stuff. We see it, we desire it, we shop for it, we put it on display, we buy insurance for it, and we compare it with other people's stuff. And celebrities are a good reminder we still don't have enough stuff because we don't have as much stuff as they have.

> How interested are you in celebrity lifestyle? Who are your favorite celebrities? What characteristics about a celebrity make them interesting or not interesting to you?

---

121 Jerome Allen "Jerry" Seinfeld (born April 29, 1954) is an American stand-up comedian, actor, writer, and television/film producer, best known for the sitcom *Seinfeld* (1989–1998). Chris Kakaras, our executive pastor, considers Jerry Seinfeld the single greatest comedian of all time and often times weaves large portions of his stand up into everyday conversation as if they were his own.

122 John Christopher "Johnny" Depp II (born June 9, 1963) is an American actor who has won both the Golden Globe Award and Screen Actors Guild award for Best Actor. Depp has starred in many movies including *Edward Scissorhands* (1990), *Sleepy Hollow* (1999), *Charlie and the Chocolate Factory* (2005), and the *Pirates of the Caribbean* film series (2003–present). Most recently, he starred as Tonto in *The Lone Ranger* (2013), which was a terrible flop, costing more than $250 million to make, but bringing in less than $88 million. However, our worship pastor Jay Hendricks thinks that *The Lone Ranger* was a good movie.

123 Kanye Omari West (born June 8, 1977) is an American hip hop musician, songwriter, record producer, film director, and fashion designer who has won a total of more than 20 Grammy awards. Kimberly Noel "Kim" Kardashian (born October 21, 1980) is an American television personality, fashion designer, model, and actress. The two have been in a relationship since April 2012 and have a daughter, North. Both have been controversial figures with Kanye making many public political statements such as "George Bush doesn't care about black people" in 2005.

124 A P-51 Mustang is an American long-range, single-seat fighter and fighter-bomber used during World War II, the Korean War and other conflicts. Cruise's Mustang is a new build of the same design and it is beautiful, although I bet he regrets naming it "Kiss Me Kate." **To see a picture of it, go to www.midtowncolumbia.com/GoodLifeLinks link #124.**

According to a three-year long research project on religion and economic values from Princeton University, eighty-nine percent of Americans agreed, "our society is much too materialistic."[125] By sheer coincidence, almost the exact same percentage of Americans said we wanted more for ourselves.

Because we all know that all those materialists out there are bad. But that's not us.

None of us thinks *we* are materialistic.

We just want a little bit more.

"In a Gallup poll, the respondents, on average, said 21 percent of Americans are rich. But only 0.5 percent said they were rich. Everybody thinks he needs one thing to make himself rich: more."[126]

None of us thinks *we* are rich.

We just want a little bit more.

In America we suffer from what Greg Easterbrook calls "abundance denial."[127] We almost always compare what we have to those who have more than us in such a way we construct elaborate ways to convince ourselves we do not have too much. After all, so-and-so down the street has a bigger boat. I would be rich if I had more like they do.

Solomon deeply understands this longing to be in the Cham-

---

125 Wuthnow, Robert. "Pious Materialism: How Americans View Faith and Money" **To read the article, go to www.midtowncolumbia.com/GoodLifeLinks link #125.**
126 Ortberg, John. *When the Game is Over, it All Goes Back in the Box* (Grand Rapids, MI: Zondervan, 2007) p. 194.
127 Gregg discusses this idea in a book entitled *The Progress Paradox: How Life Gets Better While People Feel Worse.* The basic premise of his book is an amazing scientific and cultural study of how almost every factor related to quality of life has improved in the past 50 years while our overall perception of happiness hasn't changed in the slightest. If anything our levels of depression, anxiety and dissatisfaction have increased in that time frame.

pagne Club. He lived the life of *more* beyond what any of us will ever experience. And in the midst of having as much wealth and as much stuff as he could ever want, he comes to an insightful revelation: *"He who loves money will not be satisfied with money, nor he who loves wealth with his income; this also is vanity."*[128]

> **Read 1 Timothy 6:6-10.** Paul echoes Solomon's warning about the love of money. Why does money lead some to walk away from the faith? What does Paul say is the antidote to the trap of wanting more? How difficult is it for you to walk in contentment with what you have?
>
> _____
>
> _____
>
> _____
>
> _____

MORE IS NEVER ENOUGH

Ebenezer Scrooge.[129]

Tom Walker.[130]

Ananias and Sapphira.[131]

---

128   Ecclesiastes 5:10
129   Ebenezer Scrooge is the main character in Charles Dickens's 1843 novel, *A Christmas Carol*. At the beginning of the novel, Scrooge is a cold-hearted, tight-fisted, and greedy man, until three Christmas ghosts show him how his greed is ruining his life and lead him to redemption, repentance and charity. The theological accuracy of Christmas ghosts is debated by scholars.
130   "The Devil and Tom Walker" is a short story by Washington Irving in which Tom is a greedy miser and he sells his soul to the Devil in return for a treasure hidden in a forest by Kidd the Pirate. "The Devil Went Down to Georgia" is a song by the Charlie Daniels Band that was loosely based on Irving's short story.
131   In Acts 5:1-11, a married couple in the early church sells some property to give to the church but selfishly lies about the sum of the gift and keeps some for themselves. For their greed and selfishness, they both die on the spot.

Icarus,[132] Midas,[133] and Narcissus.[134]

The dread pirate Hendrick Lucifer.

Don't know that one? Pirate Lucifer fought for hours and hours to acquire Cuban gold, becoming mortally wounded in the process. His wounds led to his demise mere hours after he finished transferring the booty to his ship.

The moral of the pirate's tale?

Beware of the tempting search for *more*.[135]

The cultural stories and anecdotes warning us about greed – both historical and mythological –are everywhere. They wave big warning flags and sound high-pitched alarms shouting, "More is never enough!"

But still we search for more.

> Where do you sense in yourself an unsatisfied quest for more?
>
> _____
>
> _____
>
> _____
>
> _____

What is fascinating is the scientific research that gladly sup-

---

[132] In Greek mythology, Icarus is the son of the master builder Daedalus. Daedalus constructs wings for him and his son and instructs his son not to fly too close to the sun. Icarus ignores his father's warning because he wants to experience more height. The sun melts his wings and he plummets to the sea below where he drowns.

[133] In Greek mythology, Midas was a king with the ability to turn anything he touched into gold. It's a cautionary tale as his vain prayer for the ability to create his own wealth eventually kills his daughter when he accidentally turns her into a gold statue.

[134] In Greek mythology, Narcissus was a hunter from the territory of Thespiae in Boeotia who was renowned for his beauty. He is lured into a trap where he falls in love with his own image reflecting in a pool. Overwhelming consumed with wanting to see more and more of his beauty Narcissus dies. This tale is a good motivator if your spouse is taking too long getting ready and looking in the mirror. Just playfully remind them, "Don't forget what happened to Narcissus honey!" Works every time.

[135] If you thought the moral of the story was, "Beware the danger of a big, tempting booty" then ten bonus points for you.

ports Solomon's observation. Dr. Ronnie Janoff Bulman and her colleagues compared three different categories of people: lottery winners, average folks, and victims of sudden paralysis.[136]

Over-time, none of the lottery winners reported higher levels of happiness or lower levels of depression than they felt before winning the lottery. Once the thrill of winning the lottery subsided, they actually lost much of their ability to appreciate and enjoy small pleasures. Shockingly, the paralysis victims retained more of their capacity to experience joy in small pleasures than the lottery winners and were also more optimistic about their opportunity for future happiness. In an article entitled "Consumerism and its Discontents", Tori DeAngelis quotes Hope College psychologist David G. Myers, PhD who describes our culture:

> "Compared with their grandparents, today's young adults have grown up with much more affluence, slightly less happiness, and much greater risk of depression and assorted social pathology... Our becoming much better off over the last four decades has not been accompanied by one iota of increased subjective well-being."[137]

DeAngelis demonstrates that more and more studies are revealing materialism and consumerism bring more dissatisfaction, less happiness, and more overall stress. One Ph.D, Edward Diener admitted having money did make materialists happier than not having money, but in perceived happiness they never caught up to non-materialists. "So if you're poor, it's very bad to be a materialist; and if you're rich, it doesn't make you happier than non-materialists, but you almost catch up."

---

136 Downie, James. *New Republic.* "Winning the Lottery or A Car Accident: Which Makes You Happier?" **To read the article, go to www.midtowncolumbia.com/GoodLifeLinks link #136.**

137 Myers, David G. "The Funds, Family and Faith of Happy People" *American Psychologist* (Vol. 55, No. 1)

Why do you think materialism and the quest for more don't pay off? Have you ever gotten the *more* you thought you need and then not been satisfied by it?

_____

_____

_____

LEARNING FROM THOSE WHO HAVE MORE THAN US

A surprising number of the rich and the famous we so often admire don't necessarily recommend being rich as a satisfying way to live.

"Money has never made man happy, nor will it. There is nothing in its nature to produce happiness. The more of it one has the more one wants."

- Benjamin Franklin[138]

"A business that makes nothing but money is a poor business. I was happier when doing a mechanic's job."

- Henry Ford[139]

"The care of $200 million is enough to kill anyone. There is

---

138 Benjamin Franklin was a successful newspaper editor and tycoon and was wealthy enough to retire from income generating work in his early forties. His face is featured on the US one hundred dollar bill. Also, "rollin' in the benjamins" is a slang phrase that describes someone being filthy rich.
139 Henry Ford was an American industrialist in the early 1900s. Although he didn't invent the automobile, he established the assembly line that made automobiles cheap and accessible to the public. He also founded the Ford Motor Company. As owner of the Ford Motor Company, he became one of the richest and best-known people in the world.

no pleasure in it."

- W.H. Vanderbilt[140]

"I have made millions, but they have brought me no happiness."

- John D. Rockefeller[141]

"Millionaires seldom smile."

- Andrew Carnegie[142]

Throughout history, many of those who have had the most have looked at those of us with less and said, "It's never enough. More will never satisfy you." And for some reason we are unable to hear them. Something in our heart remains skeptical.

"Oh that's easy for you to say because you are rich!"

But we should doubt our doubts. The rich are the only ones who are a reliable resource on whether being rich is truly satisfying or not. And from Solomon, to Vanderbilt, to Pitt, and Carrey, they all agree.[143]

---

140 William Henry Vanderbilt III was Governor of Rhode Island and a member of the wealthy and socially prominent Vanderbilt family.

141 John Davidson Rockefeller was an American industrialist, philanthropist, and oil tycoon in the early that lived from 1839-1937. He founded Standard Oil Company, which was incredibly successful. So much so, that if you adjust for inflation Rockefeller is often regarded as the richest person in history. For his hard work in revolutionizing the petroleum industry, he is honored with a huge Christmas tree next to an ice skating rink at the Rockefeller center every year at Christmas. This ice skating rink has been featured in movie classics such as *Elf*, *Serendipity*, and *Home Alone 2*.

142 Andrew Carnegie was a Scottish American industrialist who led the enormous expansion of the American steel industry in the late 19th century. In 1901 he sold his steel company for the modern equivalent of $13.2 billion. For his time he was very, very wealthy but compared to Rockefeller he was a schmuck. Therefore, he is not honored with a giant Christmas tree. He did build Carnegie Hall and he was an incredible philanthropist who called on the rich to use their money to build society so that's pretty cool.

143 We referenced similar quotes from Brad Pitt and Jim Carrey back in Chapter 2.

Being rich doesn't deliver the good life.
The good life isn't found in the Champagne Club.

> Why do you think people who are living in the Champagne Club aren't satisfied by their extreme wealth and cool stuff? Why do you think we still long to be wealthy despite their warnings?
>
> _____
>
> _____
>
> _____
>
> _____

MONEY VIEWED FROM ABOVE THE SUN

What is this insatiable longing for *more* actually telling us about ourselves?

Because almost nine out of ten of us know our society is too materialistic.

But almost none of think we have enough.

We still hunger for more.

And we can all read the research that shows us more won't make us happy.

And we still yearn for more.

What's going on inside of us?

What is wrong with us?

> Have you ever been really, really excited about getting something new only to get it and be really surprised at how quickly the thrill wears off? Do you ever notice yourself comparing yourself to those who have more than you? What is the effect in your soul?

_____

_____

_____

_____

Some of the most famous and amazing Christians who have ever lived (much better Christians than me or you) have said some of the most amazing and beautiful things about this concept.

> "It would seem that Our Lord finds our desires not too strong, but too weak. We are half-hearted creatures, fooling about with drink and sex and ambition when infinite joy is offered us, like an ignorant child who wants to go on making mud pies in a slum because he cannot imagine what is meant by the offer of a holiday at the sea. We are far too easily pleased."
>
> - C.S. Lewis, prolific Author and Genius

> "He is no fool who gives what he cannot keep to gain that which he cannot lose."
>
> - Jim Elliott, Missionary and Author

Hmmm, yes. Preach it Jim. You tell em' Clive.[144] And Solomon agrees. In some ways the whole point of Ecclesiastes is that all of our longings and attempts to find satisfaction here on earth, under the sun, are vain, utterly meaningless, unless we allow these vain temporary things to show our hearts what we really want is life with God beyond the sun.

Money is not evil.

Stuff is not evil.

---

144 The C.S. stands for Clive Staples… So now you know why he went by C.S.

But the love of money is a root of all kinds of evil.[145]

Believing money will truly satisfy our deepest desires is a fool's errand.

> *"He who loves money will not be satisfied with money, nor he who loves wealth with his income;"*[146]

Solomon asks us the haunting question, "Do you want to be able to sleep at night?" Then learn your desire for more is pointing you way beyond money and stuff. Quit believing money is going to satisfy your deepest desires. Understand work and money are both gifts from God, so work hard and use both your work and your money to glorify Him.

> Do you ever find yourself dreaming about *more* when you're trying to go to sleep? Do you see a pattern of your desire for more shifting from one thing to the next throughout your life?
>
> _____
>
> _____
>
> _____
>
> _____

WIELDING THE TOOL OF MONEY
READ ECCLESIASTES 5:13-20

Chris Kakaras, one of our pastors who oversees all of our church's finances loves to talk about how money is amoral. He often says, "It's like a brick. If I have a brick I can use it to help build an orphanage, or I can use it to throw it through someone's window. The brick is not moral. The person using the brick is moral." We

---
145 1 Timothy 6:10
146 Ecclesiastes 5:10

can only see how to wield the tool of money when we join Jesus in viewing money from above the sun.

Author and creative thinker, Seth Godin, helps to expand this idea:

> "If money is an emotional issue for you, you've just put your finger on a big part of the problem. No one who is good at building houses has an emotional problem with hammers. Place your emotional problems where they belong, and focus on seeing money as a tool.[147]

From working construction, the right tool used in the right way makes a project ten times easier. At best, the wrong tool used the wrong way only leaves you with scars and some hilarious stories. Solomon helps us lay the groundwork for how to wield the tool of our money. First he gives us the safety warnings:

1. DON'T OPPRESS THE POOR.
Read Ecclesiastes 5:8-9, Zechariah 7:10 and Isaiah 30:12-14.
Be the kind of overseer who cultivates his fields and cares about his workers. Don't cut corners. Don't take advantage of people. Don't rip people off. God doesn't take oppression lightly.

> Are you in a position of power to take care of or mistreat those under your authority? Are there any ways in which you are abusing your power and taking advantage of others?
>
> _____
>
> _____
>
> _____

---

147 Godin, Seth. "Thinking about money" **To read the article which is a short and insightful read, go to www.midtowncolumbia.com/GoodLifeLinks link #147.**

2. DON'T HOARD YOUR MONEY.
Read Ecclesiastes 5:13 and Luke 12:13-21.
There is a way to hold onto your own money in a way that harms you. There is a way to become so consumed with money you fail to be rich toward God. Don't let your money and your stuff own you.

> Are there any sneaky places where you are tempted to hoard in life?
>
> _____
> _____
> _____
> _____

3. DON'T LIVE LIKE A GAMBLER.
Read Ecclesiastes 5:14 and Proverbs 13:11.
A gambler wants more money so badly he will take any risk in order to get it. He will risk his family's well being and his own wealth to try to get more. A gambler looks for get rich quick schemes and ends up with nothing to give to his children.

> What is the biggest gamble you've taken in your life? Why are we tempted to gamble and over-risk?
>
> _____
> _____
> _____
> _____

4. DON'T BE ANXIOUS ABOUT MONEY.
Read Ecclesiastes 5:13+17, Luke 12:22-34 and Philippians 4:6-7.
Anxiety about our money reveals we do not trust God to provide as a result of our hard work. Vexation, stress and a rough night of sleep is a telltale sign we are not viewing money as a tool.

> How anxious are you about your finances? How does this reveal you aren't viewing your money from beyond the sun?
>
> _____
>
> _____
>
> _____
>
> _____

Along with giving us safety instructions and warnings, Solomon also lays some groundwork for how we can use our money to glorify God as we consider life from beyond the sun.

1. DO CULTIVATE WHAT'S BEEN ENTRUSTED TO YOU.
Read Ecclesiastes 5:9 and Proverbs 27:23-24.
Solomon says a king who cultivates his fields is good for the land in every way. The word cultivate is the same word God uses to instruct Adam for how to take care of the garden. Keep it. Dress it. Help it grow. This applies to the people and opportunities in your care. The money God has given you is a tool to serve the people God has placed around you for God's glory.

> Where might Jesus be asking you to take steps to cultivate what you have more wisely in light of eternity?
>
> _____

2. DO LEAVE SOMETHING FOR FUTURE GENERATIONS.
Read Ecclesiastes 5:14 and Proverbs 13:22.
Inheritance is an issue of some contention for many Christians. The key issue is to consider our new family as adopted children of God and not just our immediate blood family. The question Solomon is asking us is are we going to show our kids an example of wasting everything so we have nothing to give to future generations? Or are we going to live wisely and have much to give to those who come behind?

Leave an inheritance of wisdom. Leave an inheritance of generosity. Leave an inheritance of God's grace in Jesus. And leave an inheritance of cash.

> How are you planning to be a blessing to future generations?

3. DO LIVE WITH ENJOYMENT, CONTENTMENT AND THANKFULNESS.
Read Ecclesiastes 5:18-20 and 1 Timothy 6:6-10.
Solomon saw an incredibly amount of money and an incredible amount of rich people. He concludes, *"What I have seen to be good and fitting… is to enjoy [his wealth and possessions], and to accept his lot and rejoice in his toil."* Paul instructs Timothy to warn the rich to not trust in their wealth, but instead to receive their wealth as a gift

from God, to enjoy it carefully with contentment.

> Is your life marked by enjoyment, contentment, and gratitude? Why or why not? Which of these areas do you need to grow in?
>
> _____
> _____
> _____
> _____

When these safety guidelines and techniques are used, we are freed up from believing our identity is found in the stuff that we own, and we are set free to leverage our wealth and our possessions for Jesus' kingdom.

> "He who has God and everything else has no more than he who has God only."
>
> - C. S. Lewis

LIFEGROUP DISCUSSION QUESTIONS
WEEK 6: THE CHAMPAGNE CLUB

1.) If all of your possessions were piled up and destroyed, what range of emotions would you undergo? Which things could you easily live without? Which ones would sadden you deeply? Are there any things you honestly don't think you could live without?

2.) Read Ecclesiastes 5:10. Why does the love of money never satisfy? In your life have you seen the pattern of money and possessions only bringing temporary happiness and not long-lasting joy?

3.) How can we encourage each other to press into our desire for more and let it motivate us toward our need for Jesus?

4.) Read Ecclesiastes 5:13-20. Which of the four dangers are the biggest struggles for you?

What steps do you need to take to start wielding your money more wisely in light of Solomon's three encouragements?

Pray. Spend some time in prayer together as a group regarding what you've studied. Thank God for anything He's shown you about Himself and the good life. Confess to your group where you are tempted to believe *more* would satisfy your soul. Brainstorm ways as a group that you can repent by leveraging your money and your stuff to be a blessing in view of Jesus' kingdom and mission.

But all this I laid to heart, examining it all, how the righteous and the wise and their deeds are in the hand of God. Whether it is love or hate, man does not know; both are before him. It is the same for all, since the same event happens to the righteous and the wicked, to the good and the evil, to the clean and the unclean, to him who sacrifices and him who does not sacrifice. As the good one is, so is the sinner, and he who swears is as he who shuns an oath. This is an evil in all that is done under the sun that the same event happens to all. Also, the hearts of the children of man are full of evil, and madness is in their hearts while they live, and after that they go to the dead. But he who is joined with all the living has hope, for a living dog is better than a dead lion. For the living know that they will die, but the dead know nothing, and they have no more reward, for the memory of them is forgotten. Their love and their hate and their envy have already perished, and forever they have no more share in all that is done under the sun.

Go, eat your bread with joy, and drink your wine with a merry heart, for God has already approved what you do. Let your garments be always white. Let not oil be lacking on your head. Enjoy life with the wife whom you love, all the days of your vain life that he has given you under the sun, because that is your portion in life and in your toil at which you toil under the sun. Whatever your hand finds to do, do it with your might, for there is no work or thought or knowledge or wisdom in Sheol, **to which you are going.**

Ecclesiastes 9:1-10

CHAPTER SEVEN
THE FOUNTAIN OF YOUTH

THAT WRINKLE WE'RE ALL TRYING TO HIDE
READ ECCLESIASTES 9:1-6

"People spend a lot of money each year in the quest for eternal youth and beauty, and that number is only going to get bigger as younger people hope to stave off the aging process. According to TermLifeInsurance.org, the value of the industry in 2011 was estimated at $80-billion, and is set to reach $114-billion by the year 2015 if current trends continue."[148]

That wrinkle you're trying to hide, that's death creeping in.

Those few gray hairs...

That little extra sag that didn't used to be there...

That pep in your step that you lost since high school...

They're warming up your funeral bells.

They're letting you know that death is coming.

That joint pain, that arthritis, that soreness, that slowness to recover...

No matter what we do, death comes.

Where have you noticed it? Where have you seen death's impending effects creeping in on your body and your abilities? How

---

148   McCormack, Caitlyn. "Anti-aging industry set to hit $114-billion" *Yahoo News*. **To read the article, go to www.midtowncolumbia.com/GoodLifeLinks link #148.**

are you trying to hide it? How are you trying to delay it? How are you living in denial of it?

The fact we're about to spend $114 billion on the anti-aging industry would indicate we think there is some benefit, something to be gained in trying to ignore, hide and cover up the fact that death is coming.

Why do we think that?

> Ignoring the possibility of an early death, you are going to get old (some of us are closer than others). Do you ever think about that fact? What do you think about when you think about yourself as an old person? What feelings arise as you think about aging?
>
> _____
> _____
> _____
> _____
>
> **Read Proverbs 20:29.** What kinds of older people have you known (wise, angry, disconnected, generous, aloof, compassionate, etc.)? Do you tend to think highly of the elderly as those who are marked by beautiful experience and wisdom? Why or why not?
>
> _____
> _____
> _____

Have you ever thought about what kind of older person do you want to be? Are the decisions you're making now helping you become that kind of person?[149]

DEATH IS COMING.

Solomon sees no benefit in trying to hide from the wrinkles and gray hairs that tell us death is coming. Have you noticed how frequently he points out we are all going to die? (Ecclesiastes 2:15-17, 3:2, 3:19-20, 7:1-2, 8:8, 9:1-6, 11:8-9, 12:5-7)

What do you think is his goal in repeating this theme so frequently?

In our society, a growing phenomenon is described as death anxiety: "a feeling of dread, apprehension or anxiety when one thinks of the process of dying, or ceasing to 'be'."[150] Solomon says our dread, apprehension, and anxiety won't change the fact that death is coming. And neither will more makeup, Bot-ox, or hair dye.

Infatuation with youth and fear of death are not new ideas. Tales describing the Fountain of Youth have been told across the world for thousands of years. This elusive fountain appears in writings by

---

149 For a beautiful illustration of the inevitability of old age and what happens to lively, young people over time go to www.midtowncolumbia.com/GoodLifeLinks link #149.
150 Definition by Farley G.: Death anxiety. National Health Service UK. 2010, found in: Peters L, Cant R, Payne S, O'Connor M, McDermott F, Hood K, Morphet J, Shimoinaba K. (2013). "How death anxiety impacts nurses' caring for patients at the end of life: a review of literature."

Herodotus, the Alexander romance, and the stories of the indigenous peoples of the Caribbean. The legend was also attached to the Spanish explorer Juan Ponce de León, who was searching for the Fountain of Youth when he traveled to what is now Florida in 1513. Even the Nazis are searching for the Fountain of Youth in *Indiana Jones and the Last Crusade*.[151]

Why would such a particular legend show up in so many different cultures, places, and times throughout human history?

Ernest Becker wrote a book entitled *The Denial of Death*, in which he proposes, "the idea of death, the fear of it, haunts the human animal like nothing else." Columbia University Professor, Andrew Delbanco, explains that all cultures are marked by "a lurking suspicion that all [of life] amounts to nothing more than fidgeting while we wait for death."

British philosopher and theologian, Paul Helm writes, "The modern Western attitude to dying and death is all too obvious. It is to avoid it, to avoid mentioning it, and where mention of it is unavoidable, to use euphemisms and circumlocutions."

Woody Allen adds, "It's not that I'm afraid to die. I just don't want to be there when it happens."

> How afraid are you of death? Do you agree with Becker that it is the single greatest fear that haunts humans? Where do you see examples in culture or in your life of what Helm describes as avoiding death and using euphemisms to talk about it?
>
> _____
>
> _____
>
> _____
>
> _____

---

151 The historical accuracy of this documentary is debated by scholars.

Our fear of death and desire to not think about our coming death is very peculiar. Death feels incredibly unnatural to us but it is one of the few events that have literally happened to every human who has ever lived.

But because we don't want to think about death…

What we used to call graveyards…

Now we call 'memorial gardens'.

Where we used to put skulls and crossbones on tombs to warn the living…

Now we put, "forever in our hearts."

Emphasizing the part of the person still living.

Deemphasizing the simple fact they are dead.

Some have even said we paint up our dead like clowns because we don't want to see what they look like dead. Embalming and death cosmetology have become huge industries that shield of us from the observing the physical effects that death has on a human body.

We don't want to remember them that way.

Or we don't want to deal with the reality…

That they aren't alive anymore.

In a scathing look at American funerals, *The American Way of Death*, author Joan Mitford cites a recent survey that said 75% of mortuary customers are unhappy with the appearance of the deceased. Did they expect death to have a positive effect on how their loved ones look?

Despite our fears, Solomon is showing us that trying to hide from, cover up, ignore, deny, or postpone death is futile. It doesn't get us anywhere. We all die. Death comes for all of us.

> *"The same event happens to the righteous and the wicked, to the good and the evil, to the clean and the unclean, to him who sacrifices and him who does not sacrifice. As the good one is, so is the*

sinner, and he who swears is as he who shuns an oath."[152]

Under the sun, death is terrifying so we try to avoid it, but Solomon exposes that this is utterly foolish. An infected rash doesn't heal by putting a band-aid on it so you can't see it anymore. Ignoring the fact you are going to die doesn't actually do anything to change the fact you are going to die. Out of sight, out of mind is not a helpful mentality when it comes to death.

We miss out on all the wisdom our impending death wants to give us.

WHAT DOES OUR FEAR REVEAL ABOUT HUMANITY?

What if our fear and anxiety about death were trying to tell us something about the human soul? Dr. Joseph A. Pipa, a member of Ligonier Ministries, writes:

> "Death is the great obscenity of our age. Men and women will air their sex lives and other intimate details on television talk shows, but they will not talk about death... The Bible, on the other hand, speaks openly and often about death. According to the Bible, we fear death because it is unnatural. God made man in His image and gave him an immortal soul. Man wants to live forever, but death abruptly terminates his conscious physical existence."[153]

Thomas Aquinas came to this same understanding by studying Augustine and the metaphysics of Aristotle. In his *Summa Theologiae*, Aquinas writes, "Death is natural as regards matter [the destructible body] but not as regards form [the indestructible soul]."

Have you ever thought about the fact that according to the Bible

---

[152] Ecclesiastes 9:2
[153] Pipa, Joseph. *Ligonier Ministries.* "Faces of Death". **To read the article, go to www.midtowncolumbia.com/GoodLifeLinks link #153.**

death is not natural to human existence?

Death was not part of God's original design for humans. Death is a result of the curse and the fall.[154]

What's interesting is that some scientists who don't accept theological explanations have come to this same conclusion that death is unnatural. Arthur Caplan, Director of the Center for Bioethics at the University of Pennsylvania, explains:

> "[We all assume] that aging is a common and normal process. It occurs with a statistical frequency of 100%. Inevitably, bones become brittle, vision dims, joints stiffen and muscles lose their tone. The obvious question then is whether commonality, familiarity, and inevitability are sufficient conditions for labeling certain biological states as natural…"

After arguing why commonality, familiarity and inevitability are all insufficient to label certain biological states as natural, Caplan concludes:

> "The explanation of why aging occurs has many of the attributes of a chance phenomenon. And this makes aging unnatural and in no way an intrinsic part of human nature."[155]

> What are the implications if death is actually an unnatural part of human existence? Does this idea change or help you understand how you think and feel about death?

---

154 God specifically names death as part of the curse in Genesis 3:19. *"By the sweat of your face you shall eat bread till you return to the ground, for out of it you were taken; for you are dust, and to dust you shall return."*
155 Caplan, Arthur. *EMBO Reports*. "Death as an unnatural process" **To read the article, go to www.midtowncolumbia.com/GoodLifeLinks link #155.**

_____

_____

_____

_____

Read Revelation 21:4. Jesus shows John a vision of heaven where death is no longer part of the human experience. What impact does that thought have on your soul?

_____

_____

_____

_____

SEIZING THE DAY IN LIGHT OF ETERNITY
READ ECCLESIASTES 9:7-10

In the 1989 movie, *Dead Poet's Society*, while staring at a trophy case of impressive accomplishments and photographs of previous students, English professor John Keating gives a rousing and rallying speech to his literature students:

> "They're not that different from you, are they? Same haircuts. Full of hormones, just like you. Invincible, just like you feel. The world is their oyster. They believe they're destined for great things, just like many of you; their eyes are full of hope, just like you. Did they wait until it was too late to make from their lives even one iota of what they were capable? Because, you see gentlemen, these boys are now fertilizing daffodils.

Insight from Ecclesiastes

But if you listen real close, you can hear them whisper their legacy to you. Go on. Lean in. You hear it? (whispering) carpe – hear it? – carpe – carpe diem. Seize the day boys. Make your lives extraordinary."

This philosophy of *carpe diem*, Latin for "seize the day", shows up throughout our culture. From Nike's, "Just Do It",[156] to Dave Matthews singing, "Eat, drink and be merry, for tomorrow you die",[157] to the ever present YOLO.[158] In Christopher Nolan's Oscar-winning movie *Inception*, one of his characters sums this up perfectly when he asks, "Do you want to take a leap of faith or become an old man filled with regret waiting to die alone?"[159]

They are all echoing Solomon's thoughts in Ecclesiastes 9.

Life is short.

You're going to die.

So enjoy your life while you can: here and now.

But is that it? Is it just enjoying life under the sun and then you die and that's all?

Or does the ability to anticipate our death have profound impact on the way we live? An even deeper and more profound impact than putting a 'live, laugh, love!' painting on our wall?

Jonathan Edwards, the theologian who in many ways led the Great Awakening, famously wrote a series of inspiring *Resolutions*. One of which was *"to think much on all occasions of my own dying, and*

---

[156] Many have pointed to Nike's "Just do it" campaign as one of the most successful of all time. AdWeek recently called it the Last Great advertising campaign. **To read the article, go to www.midtowncolumbia.com/GoodLifeLinks link #156.**

[157] Dave Matthews is the front man for the popular 90s jam band, The Dave Matthews Band. He sings "Eat, drink and be merry for tomorrow you die" on the song "Tripping Billies", the fifth single from their album *Crash*. This phrase is a combination of Ecclesiastes 8:15 and Isaiah 22:13.

[158] YOLO stands for You Only Live Once. Also, the boys from Lonely Island made a hilarious video that reinterprets YOLO that you can watch here: **go to www.midtowncolumbia.com/GoodLifeLinks link #158.**

[159] Saito asks this question to Cobb to convince him to try the main inception that drives the entire plot even though Cobb has no guarantee that it's going to work.

of the common circumstances which attend death."[160]

Edwards spent a lot of time thinking about his death.

He intentionally chose to do so.

Edward's conclusion and motive in thinking much on his own dying was not simply to enjoy life under the sun more fully. Instead, Edwards saw life from above the sun and used meditating on his own death to motivate his passion to preach the gospel and to impact as many as possible for eternal life beyond the grave. It helped him to live each day with intentionality and to prioritize the things that matter.

> **Read Philippians 1:20-24.** How did Paul consider his life and death? In light of your inevitable death, how much do you long to depart and be with Christ? In what ways do you practically see fruitful ministry as the primary purpose of your life?
>
> _____
>
> _____
>
> _____
>
> _____

Solomon's reality is our reality.

None of us make it out of this life alive.

But the inevitability of death doesn't have to be depressing.

It doesn't have to send us running to Avon or Mary Kay for camouflage.

It doesn't have to send us searching for the Fountain of Youth.

Because in Jesus there is a real fountain of living water.

And He has invited us to drink deeply for free.[161]

---

[160] You can read an abbreviated version of Jonathan Edward's complete list of Resolutions here: **go to www.midtowncolumbia.com/GoodLifeLinks link #160.**
[161] John 4:7-15, John 7:37-38, Revelation 7:15-17, Revelation 21:6

He has invited us to see our lives and our deaths from His perspective beyond the sun.

And when we see how short life is in light of our inevitable death...

When we see how Jesus has conquered death...

We are compelled by His grace and love to leverage our lives in light of eternity for His mission and His kingdom and life with Him forever.

> "Human beings are the only creatures whose frontal lobes are so developed that they know that the game will end. This is our glory, our curse, our warning, and our opportunity.
>
> - John Ortberg

LIFEGROUP DISCUSSION QUESTIONS
WEEK 7: THE FOUNTAIN OF YOUTH

1.) What portion of the sermon or study guide stood out the most to you? How much do you think about your own death? How much effort do you put into avoiding, ignoring, and postponing the effects of death in your life?

_____

_____

_____

_____

_____

2.) Read 1 Corinthians 15:50-58.
What do you think of Solomon's pessimistic view of death under the sun? Is he right that death and being forgotten renders our lives under the sun as meaningless?

_____

_____

_____

_____

_____

If we could see from over the sun, how would it impact our perspective on death? How does the gospel change Solomon's pessimism about death?

Insight from Ecclesiastes

3.) Read Ecclesiastes 3:19-21 and 9:7-10. How does the reality of your coming death effect your contentment, your enjoyment of life, and how you use your life now? What does seizing the day look like in your world?

Pray: Ask Jesus to help us see life is short. Ask Him to free us from our fear and hiding from death. Ask Him to help us rejoice in His conquering of the grave. Ask Him to help us leverage our lives for His kingdom in light of death that is coming.

LifeGroup Challenge: As individuals or as a group, go to a graveyard. Reflect for 20 minutes on the reality of death and how to view life from above the sun in light of your coming death. Print out and read Edward's *Resolutions* if it is helpful.[162]

---

[162] Go here to get the Resolutions link: **www.midtowncolumbia.com/GoodLife-Links link #162**.

Rejoice, O young man, in your youth, and let your heart cheer you in the days of your youth. Walk in the ways of your heart and the sight of your eyes. But know that for all these things God will bring you into judgment. Remove vexation from your heart, and put away pain from your body, for youth and the dawn of life are vanity.

Remember also your Creator in the days of your youth, before the evil days come and the years draw near of which you will say, "I have no pleasure in them"; before the sun and the light and the moon and the stars are darkened and the clouds return after the rain, in the day when the keepers of the house tremble, and the strong men are bent, and the grinders cease because they are few, and those who look through the windows are dimmed, and the doors on the street are shut—when the sound of the grinding is low, and one rises up at the sound of a bird, and all the daughters of song are brought low— they are afraid also of what is high, and terrors are in the way; the almond tree blossoms, the grasshopper drags itself along, and desire fails, because man is going to his eternal home, and the mourners go about the streets— before the silver cord is snapped, or the golden bowl is broken, or the pitcher is shattered at the fountain, or the wheel broken at the cistern, and the dust returns to the earth as it was, and the spirit returns to God who gave it. Vanity of vanities, says the Preacher; all is vanity.

Besides being wise, the Preacher also taught the people knowledge, weighing and studying and arranging many proverbs with great care. The Preacher sought to find words of delight, and uprightly he wrote words of truth.

The words of the wise are like goads, and like nails firmly fixed are the collected sayings; they are given by one Shepherd. My son, beware of anything beyond these. Of making many books there is no end, and much study is a weariness of the flesh.

The end of the matter; all has been heard. Fear God and keep his commandments, for this is the whole duty of man. For God will bring every deed into judgment, with every secret thing, whether good or evil.

Ecclesiastes 11:8-10 + 12:1-14

CHAPTER EIGHT
JOY, SATISFACTION & THE FEAR OF GOD

THE JOY WE ARE REALLY CHASING
READ ECCLESIASTES 12:1-7

Scott Adams, an American cartoonist who created the widely successful Dilbert cartoon[163], once commented on the human condition: "Free will is an illusion. People always choose the perceived path of greatest pleasure." Adams' point is that our drive for pleasure is the subconscious motive in everything we do. Blaise Pascal, a seventeenth century mathematical genius and theologian, reinforces and expounds on Adam's idea:

> "All men seek happiness. This is without exception. Whatever different means they employ, they all tend to this end. The cause of some going to war, and of others avoiding it, is the same desire in both, attended with different views. The will never takes the least step but to this object. This is the motive of every action of every man, even of those who hang themselves."

---

163 Dilbert cartoons are extremely dry and sarcastic print cartoons that illustrate much of the boring and ridiculous nature of life in an average office environment. **For an example, go to** www.midtowncolumbia.com/GoodLifeLinks **link #163.**

> Do you agree with Adams and Pascal? Are there any places where you don't believe humans are motivated by the desire for pleasure?

Bookending the entire book of Ecclesiastes, Solomon once again highlights his theme of the meaningless pursuit of happiness under the sun. In the first two chapters of Ecclesiastes, Solomon outlined his overall experiment in life – testing every common pursuit of happiness – and his incredible conclusion that none of these are truly satisfying. Here as he comes to the end of the book, he concludes by encouraging us to seek ultimate happiness in God, the eternal source and creator of happiness. He warns us that if we look for joy outside of God, we will inevitably come to his same bitter and frustrated conclusion in our old age.

> **Read Ecclesiastes 11:8-12:1** What commands and encouragements does Solomon give? Why do you think he encourages us to embrace, rejoice in and be cheered in our youth?

Like much of the Proverbs that are addressed as training manuals to a son,[164] here at the end of Ecclesiastes, Solomon is giving his parting thoughts as a wise parent. In v. 9, Solomon tells us to *"Walk in the ways of your heart and in the sight of your eyes."* He is literally instructing us to participate in the same experiment he tried. It's a direct mirror of what he said in Ecclesiastes 2:10 – *"And whatever my eyes desired I did not keep from them. I kept my heart from no pleasure..."* In light of Ecclesiastes' main message that every pursuit of happiness is ultimately meaningless, it seems strange Solomon would tell us to engage in the same kind of experiment he pursued. But there is one important catch. Solomon ends vs. 9 with a specific warning.

> *"But know that for all these things God will bring you into judgment."*[165]

He echoes this somber warning with his final concluding thought:

> *"Fear God and keep his commandments, for this is the whole duty of man. For God will bring every deed into judgment, with every secret thing, whether good or evil."*[166]

As modern intellectual Americans, immediately we start to wonder why we spent all this time reading and studying this book. Solomon's parting thought is fear God because He's going to judge us? That doesn't seem right. Throughout this final chapter we will unpack what Solomon means by his last parting piece of wisdom.

> What do you think when you hear the words, "the fear of God"? Would you say you know a good bit about what the Bible says on the topic and you

---

164　See Proverbs 1:8-10.
165　Ecclesiastes 11:9
166　Ecclesiastes 12:13-14

naturally agree with the idea? Why or why not? Do you feel like the command to fear God conflicts with other truths you know about God?

_____

_____

_____

_____

If you are like most people in our culture, you probably recoil at the idea of fearing God. We tend to not quickly embrace the fire and brimstone image of an angry man in the sky raining down lightning bolts of judgment (although the Bible does at comes frighteningly close to describing God's righteous judgment in those terms).[167] Part of the problem here is we don't have a very full understanding of fear.

GOOD FEAR AND BAD FEAR
READ ECCLESIASTES 12:13-14.

Author and speaker, Christine Louise Hohlbaum, explains the dual nature of good and bad fear in an article entitled *The Benefits of Fear:* "Fear is a tricky human emotion. It can paralyze you. It can keep you small. It can also keep you safe. Fear can be your friend in just the right doses..."[168]

Bad fear paralyzes you in illogical ways. Good fear keeps you from slapping a cop in the face for no reason. Bad fear makes you paranoid that the urban legend about spiders crawling in your mouth while you sleep may actually be true.[169] Good fear keeps you

---

167 Genesis 19:24, Psalm 11:6, Matthew 13:41-43, Revelation 21:8
168 Hohlbaum, Christine Louise. *Psychology Today.* "The Benefits of Fear" **To Read the article, go to www.midtowncolumbia.com/GoodLifeLinks link #168.**
169 In case this urban legend is particularly frightening to you, you can Google search the question, "Do people eat 8 spiders a year while they're sleeping?" or you can just

from playing foursquare in the middle of the highway.

Kelly McGonigal, a Ph.D. health psychologist at Stanford University explains, "Few of us know what it's like to be unburdened by fear. We imagine it would make us bolder and braver. In reality, it would make us stupider. Fear, as it turns out, is a fundamental part of making good decisions."[170]

Scientists have a difficult time explaining exactly how fear functions in our mind, with many brain studies showing fear activating multiple portions of our brain simultaneously. However Ralph Adolphs, Ph.D and professor of psychology and neuroscience at CalTech has determined that "the amygdala is prominently activated across studies of fear."[171] The funny thing about the amygdala is that it is a fairly underdeveloped portion of our brain that can produce a wide variety of human responses. As a result, "The human body's response to fear and anxiety (stress) is exactly the same whether a threat is real or imagined."[172]

And herein lies the heart of the difference between good fear and bad fear. Good fear is an appropriate reaction to a worthy and real threat. Bad fear is an inappropriate reaction to an unworthy and/or imagined threat.

> What are your biggest fears in life? Do you have any irrational fears? Do you suffer from any phobias (spiders, dogs, heights, etc.) or paranoia? What kind of deeper-seated fears do you wrestle with (fear of rejection or abandonment, fear of failure, etc.)?

---

go read the article found at **www.midtowncolumbia.com/GoodLifeLinks link #169.**
170 McGonigal, Kelly. *Psychology Today.* "Why We Need a Little Fear" **To Read the article, go to www.midtowncolumbia.com/GoodLifeLinks link #170.**
171 Adolphs, Ralph. *The Biology of Fear.* Current Biology 23, R79–R93, January 21, 2013 a2013 Elsevier Ltd **To read the article, go to www.midtowncolumbia.com/GoodLifeLinks link #171.**
172 DeMarco, Dr. Anthony J. "The Biology of Fear and Anxiety". **To read the article, go to www.midtowncolumbia.com/GoodLifeLinks link #172.**

How do your personal fears break down into the categories of good fear and bad fear?

KEEPING GOD IN VIEW

The first thing we have to understand in Solomon's parting volley is that the fear of God means living our lives with God in view. This is absolutely foundational to Solomon's conclusion on his experiment. Every pursuit in life is meaningless and empty when we don't have God in view. In some ways the fear of God is nothing more than an accurate and an active view of God. When all-powerful, all-knowing, all-glorious God of the universe enters our field of scope, fear is the first and most natural response.

Pastor and author John Piper explains how our culture fails to keep God in view:

> "All understandings of all things that do not take God into consideration are superficial understandings, since they do not reckon with the true deepest connections with all things with what really matters in the universe, namely God. We today in America can scarcely begin to feel how God-ignor-

ing we have become because it is the very air we breathe. We breathe God-ignoring air."[173]

The issue is not only we ignore God. It's that our culture is so built on ignoring God we are almost unable to realize when we are doing it. Solomon agrees with Piper. When we breathe God-ignoring air, we lose the ability to truly understand where real satisfaction is found.

> What differences have you noticed during times when you have God in view vs. times when you don't have God in view? How do you think, feel and act differently?
>
> _____
>
> _____
>
> _____
>
> _____

Piper expounds on our God-ignoring culture by pointing to the spiritual impact of television:

> "It is a deadly place to rest the mind. Its pervasive banality, sexual innuendo, and God-ignoring values have no ennobling effects on the […] soul. It kills the spirit. It drives God away. It quenches prayer. It blanks out the Bible. It cheapens the soul. It destroys spiritual power. It defiles almost everything."

Whether or not we agree with Piper's specific view of television, he successfully illustrates how much of our common, everyday culture is a blatant distraction from keeping God in view. The goal

---

[173] Piper, John. Sermon from October 10, 2003. "A God-Entranced Vision of All Things" **To listen to the sermon or read a transcript, go to www.midtowncolumbia.com/GoodLifeLinks link #173.**

here is not that we would take a fundamentalist view that TV and everything in our culture is evil. Remember Solomon is arguing the only way to truly enjoy our lives is to keep God in our view.

The point isn't that culture is evil.

The point is that every pursuit in culture is detrimental to our joy if it steals our attention from God.

> What are the primary distractions that cause your mind and heart to ignore God? Can you think of any ways that these diversions rob your joy?
>
> _____
> _____
> _____
> _____
>
> **Read Psalm 112:1.** Where have you seen this concept revealed to be true in your life? Have you seen the fear of God and obedience to His commands leads you to the good life and deep soul level joy?
>
> _____
> _____
> _____
> _____

WE ARE NOT THE POINT

Along with leading us to keep God in view, the fear of God leads us to a deep, internal humility and understanding we are not the center of the universe. Ignoring God leads us to wrongfully believe that life is about us. We arrogantly and vainly assume that the universe spins around our desires and wishes. We assume God's role in the universe for ourselves.

Donald Miller describes this mentality with personally revealing insight in his book, *Blue Like Jazz*:

> "It is like in that movie *About a Boy* where Nick Hornby's chief character, played by Hugh Grant, believes that life is a play about himself, that all other characters are only acting minor roles in a story that centers around him.
>
> My life felt like that. Life was a story about me because I was in every scene. In fact, I was the only one in every scene. I was everywhere I went. If somebody walked into my scene, it would frustrate me because they were disrupting the general theme of the play, namely my comfort or glory. Other people were flat characters in my movie, lifeless characters. Sometimes I would have scenes with them, dialogue, and they would speak their lines, and I would speak mine. But the movie, the grand movie stretching from Adam to the Antichrist, was about me. I wouldn't have told you that at the time, but that is the way I lived."[174]

> How much do you relate to Donald Miller's idea? Do you ever find yourself thinking life is a story all about you in which everyone else is just playing a secondary role?

---

[174] Miller, Donald. *Blue Like Jazz: Nonreligious Thoughts On Christian Spirituality* (Nashville: Thomas Nelson, 2003), p. 180.

At a high school commencement, English teacher David McCullough Jr. delivered a speech that went viral almost immediately entitled "You are not special." He humorously and insightfully debunks the notion we are the point in the universe:

> "Do not get the idea that you're anything special… Even if you are 1 in a million on a planet of 6.8 billion that means there are nearly 7000 people just like you… You're planet is not the center of it's solar system. Your solar system is not the center of its galaxy. You're galaxy is not the center of the universe. In fact, astrophysicists assure us the universe has no center. Therefore, you cannot be it."[175]

This notion we are at the center of the universe – or that life is really an epic movie about our lives is radically detrimental to our search for the good life.

The more we think we are the point, the more we ignore God.

The more we think we are the point, the more annoyed we are when others mess up our movie.

The more we believe we are the point, the more miserable we will be every time the universe proves this notion is blatantly false. Author and pastor Matt Chandler explains the reality we are loved by God, but not the center of the universe:

> "God loves you, God is for you and God will provide for you,

---

[175] McCullough, David Jr. "You are not special." **To watch the video of the commencement speech, go to www.midtowncolumbia.com/GoodLifeLinks link #175.** (It really picks up at the 3:00 minute mark.)

but the motivation behind all that is not your awesomeness, but rather God. God is ultimately for God. God is about God. What God wants is the praise of God's name in the universe. It's the reason that everything exists. You, the planets, the universe, and I exist so that we might display the infinite perfections of God Almighty. Now that rubs against the air we breathe, because the air we breathe is that we're the point, we're what it's all about and everything should be about us. We breathe that air. Every commercial is pointed in that direction. 'You earned it... you deserve it... why wouldn't you?' Almost all marketing schemes are built around how worthy you are. So we said that the reality is you are not the center of God's affections. You are most definitely not the center of the universe. Ultimately God is the center of the universe."[176]

What's interesting is that the Biblical picture of the reality we are not the center of the universe is not trying to harm, belittle, or depress us. This reality actually leads us into the greatest possible, deepest level of joy. Chandler continues:

> "When the Word of God says, 'Sex is handled like this. Money is handled like this . Marriage is handled like this,' this is not God trying to flex you into a frustrated existence where He robs you of all joy. Rather it's Him leading you into the fullness of joy. The issue is you think you're smarter than God. You think know why the rules don't apply to you. And that's why I say you are your own worst enemy. No one has robbed you of joy like you have. Because you think you're smarter than God. No one has been a greater cause of misery in your

---

[176] Chandler, Matt. *The Village Church Sermons:* "Village Identity Part 2: The Mission of the Church" **To listen to the sermon, go to www.midtowncolumbia.com/GoodLifeLinks link #176.**

life than you have. You have perpetually pursued your own happiness at the detriment of your own joy."[177]

> What do you think Chandler means when he says we have pursued our happiness at the detriment of our joy? Do you agree with his claim that no one has robbed you of joy like you have? Can you see examples in your own life where you have been your own worst enemy?
>
> _____
> _____
> _____
> _____
>
> Have there been in your life times where you believed God's rules don't apply to you or that you are the exception to God's rules and His design for life? Are there any areas where that is the case currently?
>
> _____
> _____
> _____
> _____

St. Augustine once said, "Pride is the mother who is pregnant with all the other sins." All of our sin and all of our inability to live

---

[177] Chandler, Matt. *The Village Church Sermons:* "Village Identity Part 2: The Mission of the Church" and "Village Identity Part 8: God Saves" **To listen to either of these sermons, go to www.midtowncolumbia.com/GoodLifeLinks link #177.**

the good life flows from stiff-arming God and being so full of ourselves we have no room for God in us. All of our joylessness flows from believing that life is about us.

And constantly being at war with the reality that it's not.

FEARING GOD AND THE GOOD LIFE

> **Read Deuteronomy 5:29.** This verse portrays God as a parent whose heart towards His children is in anguish and pleading with them to understand His commands lead to the good life. What do you think a parent feels when their child harms themselves by ignoring their loving commands?
>
> _____
>
> _____
>
> _____
>
> _____

This picture of the fear of God leading us to the good life is a consistent pattern throughout scriptures. Proverbs 14:27 states it pretty directly: *"The fear of the LORD [is] a fountain of life, to depart from the snares of death."* Jeremiah echoes this picture of a refreshing fountain when God explains we have deserted Him in our pursuit of the good life outside of Him:

> "Has a nation changed its gods, even though they are no gods? But my people have changed their glory for that which does not profit. Be appalled, O heavens, at this; be shocked, be utterly desolate, declares the Lord, For my people have committed two evils: they have forsaken Me, the fountain of living waters, and hewed out cisterns for

themselves, broken cisterns that can hold no water."

God Himself confirms Solomon's conclusion is correct. We exchange the glory of God for that which does not profit – that which does not satisfy.

Once again Blaise Pascal, the genius mathematician, helps us understand our hearts:

> "There was once in man a true happiness of which there now remain to him only the maker and empty trace, which he in vain tries to fill from all his surroundings, seeking from things absent to help he does not obtain in things present… But these are all inadequate, because the infinite abyss can only be filled by an infinite and immutable object, that is to say, only by God Himself."

Solomon understands Pascal's point that anything less than God will never truly satisfy us because we have within us an infinite abyss. So he ends his book with an urgent, direct plea for our joy.

> "Remember also your Creator in the days of your youth, before the evil days come and the years draw near of which you will say, 'I have no pleasure in them'… The end of the matter; all has been heard. Fear God and keep his commandments, for this is the whole duty o f man. For God will bring every deed into judgment, with every secret thing, whether good or evil."[178]

Remember and fear God now.
Before it's too late.
Solomon's parting wisdom is: Go live the good life.
But understand that the good life doesn't exist without God in

---

178 Ecclesiastes 12:1 and 13-14

view.

Go search for the good life, but know that it is ultimately only found in God Himself.

Go pursue the good life, and fear God as you do.

Chase after God with reckless abandon as the true fountain of life.

And may God bless you in your chase.

LIFEGROUP DISCUSSION QUESTIONS
WEEK 8: JOY, SATISFACTION AND THE FEAR OF GOD

1.) Where in your life have you seen your pursuits of joy and happiness ultimately causes you pain?

2.) Read Ecclesiastes 11:9-10 and 12:13-14. What does it look like to pursue joy and to fear God at the same time? What do you think about the fear of God? Does it make sense to you? Do you recoil at the idea?

3.) Why do we struggle so deeply with believing we are the point of life and the center of the universe? What would it look like to encourage each other and for us to grow in repenting from this mentality?

4.) Do you agree with Solomon's assessment that it is impossible to have fullness of joy and the good life outside of God? Why or why not? Does this mean people can't live happy lives outside of relationship with God? Why or why not?

5.) Are there any areas of your life where you have been ignoring God and living life with no active awareness of God's presence? Are you pursuing joy in any hidden, unconfessed ways? Are there any areas where you believe you are an exception to God's commands? How can we encourage each other to repent and press into the good life by fearing God?

_____

_____

_____

Pray. Spend some time in prayer together as a group regarding what you've studied. Thank God for anything He's shown you about Himself and the good life. Confess to your group where you are tempted to ignore God and seek joy outside of His designs.

SECTION TWO
DAILY DEVOTIONALS

INTRODUCTION

Throughout church history, Bible study and prayer have provided the primary internal ways that Christians have cultivated deep personal love for Jesus, His family, and His mission.[1] Ecclesiastes can often be one of the more difficult books in the Bible for Christians to study, so we put together a helpful reading plan and daily devotionals to help you digest what you are reading.

Each week has five devotionals so if you miss a day here or there you won't immediately be off track and trying to play catch-up. In each devotional, you can expect to find a passage from Ecclesiastes to read, two other related passages to read, and some combination of quotes, commentary and questions to help you reflect and apply what you are learning.

If you are new to studying Scripture, here is a simple, helpful way to approach it:

1. **Scripture** - Start by reading the scriptures for 10-15 minutes. Don't write anything down yet. Just read. Read them a few times each. Pray as you read and ask Jesus to help you focus on what He wants you to see.
2. **Observation** – After reading, take 5-10 minutes to write down anything that stands out to you. These can be simple observations. If you aren't familiar with a word, look up the

---

[1] The primary external ways that Christians cultivate deep love for Jesus are loving and serving others and living on mission.

definition. If you see a new concept, write it down. What is the passage saying? What is Jesus showing me I didn't know before?

3. **Application** – After writing down your observations, take another 5-10 minutes to write down at least one way that you can apply your observations to your life. Ask yourself, "What in my life is not aligned with the truth of this passage? Jesus, where are you asking me to grow, change, and/or repent?"

4. **Prayer** – In reality, prayer is helpful from start to finish. Start by asking Jesus to help you really connect with Him. Ask Jesus to protect you from this being a religious task to try to impress Him or others. Ask Jesus to help you understand. Finally, ask Jesus for enabling grace to help you apply what you've learned.

For each day, we will give you a place to write Observations, Applications and Prayers. If you carve out thirty minutes for each of these devotionals, at the end of this campaign you will have logged over twenty hours of personal study on one of the hardest books to understand in the Bible. For many of you, these devotionals will not provide enough content for your daily time with Jesus. For some of you, this will be the first time you've ever studied the Bible. Either way, we are praying that these devotionals will be personally encouraging as you seek to live a Jesus-centered life.

READING SCHEDULE

WEEK 1:
Day 1 – Ecclesiastes 1:1-2
Day 2 – Ecclesiastes 1:3-11
Day 3 – Ecclesiastes 1:12-18
Day 4 – Ecclesiastes 2:1-8
Day 5 – Ecclesiastes 2:9-11

WEEK 2:
Day 1 – Ecclesiastes 2:12-17
Day 2 – Ecclesiastes 2:18-23
Day 3 – Ecclesiastes 2:24-26
Day 4 – Ecclesiastes 3:1-8
Day 5 – Ecclesiastes 3:9-11

WEEK 3:
Day 1 – Ecclesiastes 3:12-15
Day 2 – Ecclesiastes 2:16-21
Day 3 – Ecclesiastes 2:22
Day 4 – Ecclesiastes 4:1-3
Day 5 – Ecclesiastes 4:4-6

WEEK 4:
Day 1 – Ecclesiastes 4:7-12

Day 2 – Ecclesiastes 4:13-16
Day 3 – Ecclesiastes 5:1-7
Day 4 – Ecclesiastes 5:7-9
Day 5 – Ecclesiastes 5:10-17

WEEK 5:
Day 1 – Ecclesiastes 5:18-20
Day 2 – Ecclesiastes 6:1-6
Day 3 – Ecclesiastes 6:7
Day 4 – Ecclesiastes 6:8-12
Day 5 – Ecclesiastes 7:1-14

WEEK 6:
Day 1 – Ecclesiastes 7:15-18
Day 2 – Ecclesiastes 7:19-29
Day 3 – Ecclesiastes 8:1-9
Day 4 – Ecclesiastes 8:10-13
Day 5 – Ecclesiastes 8:14-15

WEEK 7:
Day 1 – Ecclesiastes 8:16-17
Day 2 – Ecclesiastes 9:1-2
Day 3 – Ecclesiastes 9:3-9
Day 4 – Ecclesiastes 9:10
Day 5 – Ecclesiastes 9:11-18

WEEK 8:
Day 1 – Ecclesiastes 10:1-7
Day 2 – Ecclesiastes 10:8-20
Day 3 – Ecclesiastes 11
Day 4 – Ecclesiastes 12:1-8
Day 5 – Ecclesiastes 12:9-14

DAY 1

READ:
Ecclesiastes 1:1-2; 1 Kings 3:10-14 and 4:22-34; Philippians 3:7-9

VANITY OF VANITIES

"Free will is an illusion. People always choose the perceived path of greatest pleasure."
— Scott Adams, American cartoonist

"King Solomon's life reminds me of wisdom, wealth, women, and woes."
— Toba Beta, *My Ancestor Was an Ancient Astronaut*

In order to understand the book of Ecclesiastes, we have to understand something about the man who is teaching us. God gifted Solomon with astounding wisdom that also came with wealth, incredible success, and unimaginable pleasure. He had everything we could have ever wanted. Yet throughout Ecclesiastes, Solomon repeats his refrain that life is vanity, meaningless, empty, and nothing.

What kind of instruction would you expect from an incredibly wise, wealthy, successful tycoon? Why do you think Solomon says life is empty vanity? Do you ever feel this way? How does Paul both confirm and contrast Solomon's conclusion in Philippians 3?

- **Observation:** What is the passage saying?
- **Application:** Where is Jesus asking me to repent?
- **Prayer:** How am I asking for enabling grace to repent?

DAY 2

READ:
Ecclesiastes 1:3-11; Psalm 23:1-3; Matthew 11:28-30

THE WEARINESS OF LIFE

"All things change, and never rest. Man, after all his labor, is no nearer finding rest than the sun, the wind, or the current of the river. His soul will find no rest, if he has it not from God."

– Matthew Henry, Biblical commentator

Solomon's incredible pursuit of pleasure, new experiences, and the good life ends with a frustrated weariness and boredom. Solomon sees in nature a reflection of his own reality, as the sun, wind, and water as well as human generations seem stuck in perpetual cycles that are not ever accomplishing any real goal or purpose. He's helping us see that the repetitious boredom in our lives reveals a deeper underlying lack of purpose in our pursuits.

Where have you seen this repetitious meaningless in your life? How does Jesus give us true rest and purpose in the midst of our weariness? Is there anyone God has placed in your life who is particularly weary right now and could use some encouragement to see the hope that Jesus offers us from beyond the sun?

- **Observation:** What is the passage saying?
- **Application:** Where is Jesus asking me to repent?
- **Prayer:** How am I asking for enabling grace to repent?

DAY 3

READ:
Ecclesiastes 1:12-18; Proverbs 3:5-8; Romans 8:18-23

FIXING CROOKED

"History is an endless repetition of the wrong way of living."
— Lawrence Durrell, poet, playwright and novelist

As Solomon seeks out "all that is done under heaven", he is heartbroken by an overwhelming sense of brokenness in the world:

> *"What is crooked cannot be made straight; and what is lacking cannot be counted."*

Solomon's conclusion is two-fold:

1. The presence of evil cannot be removed from the world nor from the human heart. There are crooked aspects of us and our world we cannot straighten out no matter how hard we try.

2. There is a lingering emptiness in us and in everything that we chase after to fill us. According to Solomon, this emptiness is so pervasive that it cannot be quantified.

Where do you see crookedness in your own life that never seems to get straightened out? Do you ever feel as though you are spinning your wheels as you attempt to heal, grow, and change? According to Romans 8, how does Jesus through the Spirit assist us?

- **Observation:** What is the passage saying?
- **Application:** Where is Jesus asking me to repent?
- **Prayer:** How am I asking for enabling grace to repent?

DAY 4

READ:
Ecclesiastes 2:1-8; Psalm 16; 2 Timothy 2:22

THE PURPOSE OF PLEASURE

"Many a man thinks he is buying pleasure, when he is really selling himself to it."

– Benjamin Franklin

Solomon experiences comfort and pleasure in both quantity and quality we can barely imagine. And then he asks us a startling question: "What use is it?" We don't even have a category for this question. We inherently assume pleasure is beneficial. Solomon asks us, "Why?" Whether it's a wild party with loud music, dancing, and hilarious stories the next day, or just a relaxing evening with old friends around a campfire – either way Solomon wants to know what does it accomplish? Movies, books, plays – all enjoyable but do we really gain anything from them? Sex and romantic relationship feel great in the moment but can they really answer our soul's deepest questions? Have you ever thought about why we love pleasure without question? Is there any possibility that our pursuit of pleasure is fundamentally misguided? What does King David mean when he says that in God's right hand there are pleasures forevermore?

- **Observation:** What is the passage saying?
- **Application:** Where is Jesus asking me to repent?
- **Prayer:** How am I asking for enabling grace to repent?

DAY 5

READ:
Ecclesiastes 2:9-11; Matthew 6:19-21; 1 Corinthians 3:10-15

EMOTIONALLY ATTACHED TO OUR PROJECTS
"Your work is going to fill a large part of your life, and the only way to be truly satisfied is to do what you believe is great work. And the only way to do great work is to love what you do. If you haven't found it yet, keep looking. Don't settle. As with all matters of the heart, you'll know when you find it."
– Steve Jobs, Founder and late CEO of Apple Computers, Inc.

With his unbelievable resources, Solomon began the task of building an expansive empire. From board meetings to designing, he worked on whatever he wanted to work: building palaces, national forests, and the ancient equivalent to a water park known as Solomon's pools. At the end of his toil, he disagreed with Steve Job's encouragement that "the only way to be truly satisfied is to do what you believe is great work." Solomon never did any work he didn't think was pure joy to his heart (v. 10) and still at the end of the day he realizes all his work is empty (v. 11)

Do you believe your work or projects can satisfy the deep question of your soul? Are you consistently discontent and dreaming of a better job that would deliver the good life to you? Think of the best projects you've worked on in your entire life. Did they bring lasting satisfaction? Why or why not?

- **Observation:** What is the passage saying?
- **Application:** Where is Jesus asking me to repent?
- **Prayer:** How am I asking for enabling grace to repent?

DAY 6

READ:
Ecclesiastes 2:12-17; Psalm 103:10-18; Matthew 16:24-25

MOTIVATED BY OUR MORTALITY

"We're all going to die, all of us, what a circus! That alone should make us love each other but it doesn't. We are terrified and flattened by trivialities, we are eaten up by nothing."

– Charles Bukowski, American novelist and poet

After considering that both the wisest man on earth and the biggest fool on earth both die and get buried in the ground, Solomon hits rock bottom. Staring death in the face, Solomon says he "hated life, because what is done under the sun was grievous to me, for all is vanity and a striving after wind." (v. 17)

Bukowski, however, strikes on a similar thought that Jesus teaches in Matthew 16. Solomon is right that the harder we chase after our own pleasure and selfishness the more meaningless life becomes. Jesus encourages us therefore to give our lives away for His sake that we might, "find our lives."

How can the reality of your morality spur you to give your life to others? How does Jesus' sacrificial love encourage you to find your life, not by seeking your own pleasure and selfishness, but by seeking the welfare of others for Jesus' sake?

- **Observation:** What is the passage saying?
- **Application:** Where is Jesus asking me to repent?
- **Prayer:** How am I asking for enabling grace to repent?

DAY 7

READ:
Ecclesiastes 2:18-23; Psalm 63:1-8; Matthew 5:2-12

MY FLESH FAINTS

"Jesus was broken at the cross. He lived his suffering and death not as an evil to avoid at all costs but as a mission to embrace. We too are broken. We live with broken bodies, broken hearts, broken minds, or broken spirits. We suffer broken relationships. How can we live in our brokenness? Jesus invites us to embrace our brokenness as he embraced the cross and live it as part of our mission. He asks us not to reject our brokenness as a curse from God that reminds us of our sinfulness but to accept it and put it under God's blessings for purification and sanctification. Thus, our brokenness can become a gateway to new life."

-Henry Nouwen, author of *The Wounded Healer*

As Solomon realizes the emptiness of all his pursuits in life, he's left with a deep soul restlessness: "Even in the night his heart does not rest." (v. 23) King David experiences a similar restlessness in Psalm 63 – "my flesh faints for you" – but uses his pain to send him running to God. Jesus encourages us that blessed are the spiritually weak, broken, and hungry – for they are the most ready to receive God's provision.

Are there any areas where you are currently experiencing pain or brokenness that is leading to restless nights (personal, relational, circumstantial)? How can your pain point you toward your need for Jesus?

- **Observation:** What is the passage saying?
- **Application:** Where is Jesus asking me to repent?
- **Prayer:** How am I asking for enabling grace to repent?

DAY 8

READ:
Ecclesiastes 2:24-26; Hebrews 11:1-3; Matthew 7:7-11

SEEING BEYOND THE SUN

"...Faith sees God behind all the blessings and imperfect works, which tend to conceal him, and it holds the soul in a state of continued suspense. Faith seems to keep us constantly up in the air, never quite certain of what is going to happen in the future, never quite able to touch a foot on solid ground. But faith is willing to let God act with the most perfect freedom, knowing that we belong to Him, and are to be concerned only about being faithful in that which he has given us to do for the moment."
— Francois Fenelon, Author and monk

At the end of chapter 2, Solomon gives us a breath of fresh air—acknowledging the beauty of quiet contentment found in enjoying what God has given to you. He points to faith that sees God's hand at work as a requirement in order to live the good life, "for apart from him who can eat or who can have enjoyment?" (v. 25) Solomon is saying that without understanding God as a loving Father and the giver of all good gifts, we can never receive the gifts in their proper context or enjoy them fully as evidences of God's love.

Would you say that your life is marked by quiet contentment? In what ways do you see all that you have as a gift from beyond the sun? Are there any ways that you are trying to find satisfaction in God's gifts with no acknowledgment of God Himself?

- **Observation:** What is the passage saying?
- **Application:** Where is Jesus asking me to repent?
- **Prayer:** How am I asking for enabling grace to repent?

DAY 9

READ:
Ecclesiastes 3:1-8; Daniel 2:20-21; Matthew 6:25-27

GOD CONTROLS THE SEASONS

"Life is a journey much like marriage. The certain way to be wrong is to think you control it."
— John Steinbeck, Pulitzer prize-winning author

"To surrender is to bring your coping strategies, and all they entail and represent to God. Then you choose to trust Him to provide for the legitimate needs you have, rather than trying to meet your own needs. Your openness to approaching Him and trusting Him for your needs will depend heavily on your understanding of His grace and character. A faulty understanding of God will always result in a holding onto old ways of thinking and behaving."
— Keith Miller, Author of *A Hunger for Healing*

Solomon begins the third chapter of Ecclesiastes with one of the most famous passages in all of Scripture. His humble observation is that the many seasons of life come and go and each has its place under the sun. In v. 11, He adds that God controls the seasons and "has made everything beautiful in its time."

Are there any places where it is currently hard to surrender to God's control of the seasons in your life? Do you sense any places in your soul where you are trying to control your life instead of surrendering to God's control?

- **Observation:** What is the passage saying?
- **Application:** Where is Jesus asking me to repent?
- **Prayer:** How am I asking for enabling grace to repent?

DAY 10

READ:
Ecclesiastes 3:9-11; Isaiah 43:1-7; John 4:13-14

BUSY SEARCHING FOR GOD

"Busyness is not the supreme virtue, and sanctity is not measured by the amount of work we accomplish. Virtue is found in the purity of our love for God, and this pure love is a delicate plant that grows best where there is plenty of time for it to grow and mature. In trying to turn out too much work for God, we may well end up by doing nothing for Him at all and losing our interior life at the same time. God has no need of our works...."

– Thomas Merton, Monk and author

Solomon acknowledges that God is in control of all of the seasons of life, making everything beautiful in it's own time. But Solomon also sees an inability to comprehend this reality in the hearts of men (v. 11). We end up busying ourselves with the task of trying to fill an eternity-sized abyss in our hearts. Chesterton says this drive is what sends men to the brothel. We long to be fulfilled, but nothing on earth is up for the task.

How busy are you? Do you ever take enough downtime to question whether or not your pursuits are really bringing your soul deep satisfaction? How can you break free from the busyness and let Jesus fill your eternal thirst?

- **Observation:** What is the passage saying?
- **Application:** Where is Jesus asking me to repent?
- **Prayer:** How am I asking for enabling grace to repent?

DAY 11

READ:
Ecclesiastes 3:14-15; Matthew 6:19-20, 30-33; Hebrews 12:26-28

THE UNSHAKABLE KINGDOM

"A life of worship that reverently obeys God demonstrates the unshakable presence of the kingdom of which we are citizens."

- R.C. Sproul, Founder of Ligonier Ministries

Concluding his thoughts and observations on God's control of the seasons of life, Solomon finds rest in a beautiful realization: *"I perceived that whatever God does endures forever; nothing can be added to it, nor anything taken from it"* (v. 14). King Solomon realizes that fearing God and joining Him in His work attaches our fragile lives to the anchor of Jesus' unshakable kingdom.

There are moments in all of our lives when we are shaken. There are relationships we enjoy for a time, endeavors we pursue briefly, and positions we fill that seem rock solid in the moment, but eventually are shaken and crumble. Solomon, Jesus, and the author of Hebrews all tell us that God's kingdom is different from our vulnerable, shakable lives. How have you seen God's kingdom prove to be unshakable in your life? How does the idea of God's unshakable kingdom comfort, encourage, and/or challenge you?

- **Observation:** What is the passage saying?
- **Application:** Where is Jesus asking me to repent?
- **Prayer:** How am I asking for enabling grace to repent?

DAY 12

READ:
Ecclesiastes 3:16-21; 2 Corinthians 5:1-8; 1 Corinthians 15:54-58

OUR INEVITABLE DESTINATION

"No one wants to die. Even people who want to go to heaven don't want to die to get there. And yet death is the destination we all share. No one has ever escaped it."

- Steve Jobs

"All come from dust and to dust will return". Solomon observes that just as man's physical body was made from the dust of the earth (Genesis 2:7), man's physical body will also return to dust because of the curse (Genesis 3:19). Do you ever think about the fact that you will die someday? How do you feel about that inevitable destination?

Paul writes to the church in Corinth and describes our dying physical body as a burdensome tent, almost like a hermit crab's shell. Why as a Christian can we look forward to death? In light of the gospel, what mixture of feelings and thoughts do you have toward death?

- **Observation:** What is the passage saying?
- **Application:** Where is Jesus asking me to repent?
- **Prayer:** How am I asking for enabling grace to repent?

DAY 13

READ:
Ecclesiastes 3:22; Deuteronomy 8:11-18; Colossians 3:23-24

THE FREEDOM TO ENJOY YOUR WORK

"It is our best work that God wants, not the dregs of our exhaustion. I think he must prefer quality to quantity."
            - George MacDonald – Scottish author, poet, minister

"Your work is a very sacred matter. God delights in it, and through it he wants to bestow his blessing on you. This praise of work should be inscribed on all tools, on the forehead, and faces that sweat from toiling. "
            - Martin Luther, leader of the Protestant Reformation

Solomon gets a glimmer of the reality that viewed from beyond the sun work can be seen as a gracious gift, and not a meaningless bore. Before sin entered the picture, work was not a burden, but a privilege (Genesis 2:15). Solomon, Moses (author of Deuteronomy), and Paul (author of Colossians) all see a way to view our work from over the sun – infused with Jesus' provision, grace, and oversight.

In what ways are you rejoicing in your work? In what ways do you work as if working for the Lord in all circumstances? Why do you view your work the way that you do? How can you allow the gospel to impact your thoughts, feelings, and actions regarding work?

- **Observation:** What is the passage saying?
- **Application:** Where is Jesus asking me to repent?
- **Prayer:** How am I asking for enabling grace to repent?

DAY 14

READ:
Ecclesiastes 4:1-3; Deuteronomy 10:17-19, 15:7-11; 1 John 3:17-18

OBSERVING OPPRESSION

"He that would make his own liberty secure, must guard even his enemy from oppression; for if he violates this duty, he establishes a precedent that will reach to himself."

— Thomas Paine, American Revolutionary

Solomon is staggered as he turns his wisdom and gaze to consider oppression in the world. The blatant brokenness evident in the ever-increasing ways that humans find to harm each other is almost too much for him to handle. On top of the horrendous nature of the oppression, the oppressed have no one to comfort them in their pain. The wise king muses that it would be better to be dead and even better to never be born at all than to have to really consider the reality of human inflicted suffering.

Does your heart ever break for those who are oppressed? Are there any specific causes that are particularly dear to you (poverty, sex-trafficking, single moms, clean water, etc.)? Are there any areas – locally or globally – where you can fight for or provide for the needs of the oppressed in the way Jesus fought for and provided for us in the cross?

- **Observation:** What is the passage saying?
- **Application:** Where is Jesus asking me to repent?
- **Prayer:** How am I asking for enabling grace to repent?

DAY 15

READ:
Ecclesiastes 4:4-6; Philippians 2:1-5; James 3:14-16

THE GREEN EYED MONSTER

"Envy is the art of counting the other fellow's blessings instead of your own."

- Harold Coffin

Solomon looks at human motivation for work and concludes, *"all labor and all achievement spring from man's envy of his neighbor"* (v. 4). We are envious of what others have and what they have accomplished, so we work hard to try to achieve what they have. We are envious of other's respect and approval, so we work hard trying to earn it. In the midst of this rat race, Jesus is begging us to come find perfect approval in Himself so we can be freed up to love others and consider their interests.

How are you motivated by wanting to achieve the same (or more) success as people around you? How are you motivated by wanting other people to see and be impressed by what you've done? How does Jesus challenge your envy-based motivations? How does the gospel set you free from needing to compete with or impress others?

- **Observation:** What is the passage saying?
- **Application:** Where is Jesus asking me to repent?
- **Prayer:** How am I asking for enabling grace to repent?

DAY 16

READ:
Ecclesiastes 4:7-12; Matthew 12:46-50; Hebrews 10:19-25

OVERCOMING THE FEAR OF COMMUNITY

"Either we can live as unique members of a connected community, experiencing the fruit of Christ's life within us, or we can live as terrified, demanding, self-absorbed islands, disconnected from community and desperately determined to get by with whatever resources we brought to our island with us."

–Dr. Larry Crabb, psychologist, author, Bible teacher

Throughout this passage Solomon encourages us to beware of working ourselves to death for no one and then encourages us with beautiful pictures of the blessing of living in community. But at some point we have to ask— Why does Solomon feel the need to convince us to partake in God's design for us to live communal lives? Steinbeck and Crabb present us with the reality in our souls that Solomon is fighting against. We are terrified of living vulnerable, open, dependent lives.

Where have you seen fear be an obstacle to community in your life, your family, and/or your LifeGroup? How does the author of Hebrews connect our fearless approach to the throne of God because of Jesus' grace and our pursuit of community? Why does Jesus' grace enable us to overcome our fears of each other?

- **Observation:** What is the passage saying?
- **Application:** Where is Jesus asking me to repent?
- **Prayer:** How am I asking for enabling grace to repent?

DAY 17

READ:
Ecclesiastes 4:13-16; Luke 22:24-27; Acts 17:21

FIFTEEN MINUTES OF FAME

"People are never long easy and satisfied; there is no end, no rest, of all the people; they are continually fond of changes, and know not what they would have. This is no new thing, but it has been the way of all that have been before them; there have been instances of this in every age."
— Matthew Henry, English commentator on the Bible

Solomon shares a rags-to-riches story about a poor young boy who moves from prison all the way to the throne by becoming a king. When he accomplished his quest, he lost his humble drive and *"no longer knew how to take advice."* Initially, the people embraced his success story with excitement and support, but over time his story was forgotten, and the king became an afterthought.

Are you like the king? Are there any areas of your life where you have reached success and lost your humble drive? Are you forgetting how to take advice and how to serve?

Are you like the people in the kingdom? Are you obsessed with flavor of the month, inspirational success stories? Do you find yourself moving from new thing to new thing in the chase for adrenaline and excitement?

- **Observation:** What is the passage saying?
- **Application:** Where is Jesus asking me to repent?
- **Prayer:** How am I asking for enabling grace to repent?

DAY 18

READ:
Ecclesiastes 5:1-7; John 10:27-29; James 1:19

HUMBLY LISTENING TO GOD

"I like to listen. I have learned a great deal from listening carefully. Most people never listen."

-Ernest Hemingway, author

"Wisdom is the reward you get for a lifetime of listening when you'd have preferred to talk."

-Doug Larson

In this passage, Solomon offers some humbling perspective on how we approach God. We tend to be quick to speak, rattling off a list of things we want God to do for us. Solomon encourages us to shut our mouths and approach God with humility. This makes sense if we think about someone we admire, respect, and love being near – an expert on life or an expert on something we are passionate about. If we got the chance to spend a block of time with that person, would we spend all our time talking about us? How would we approach them and try to gain some of their wisdom?

Take a moment to think about how you approach God. How would you describe your heart when you approach God? What would it look like to approach God with a heart ready to receive what He wants to say to you? Confess, repent, and ask God to set your heart on Him and give you spiritual ears to hear Him speak.

- **Observation:** What is the passage saying?
- **Application:** Where is Jesus asking me to repent?
- **Prayer:** How am I asking for enabling grace to repent?

DAY 19

READ:
Ecclesiastes 5:8-9; Deuteronomy 10:17-19; Psalm 34:18; Matthew 25:42-45

GOD'S HEART FOR THE OPPRESSED

"When men don't fear God, they give themselves to evil."
—Ray Comfort, author of *The Way of the Master*

Solomon has already noted that in a broken world oppression perpetuates itself. People with power, wealth, and position exploit those with none. For many, this kind of suffering is a reason to doubt God's goodness. But throughout the Scriptures, God is portrayed as being heartbroken by the oppression He witnesses on earth. Oppression is never God's hope for how we treat each other. Jesus goes as far as to say that when we neglect to take care of those who are in need, it as if we are directly neglecting Jesus.

Where is Jesus giving you opportunities to use your power, wealth, and position to serve those who don't have any? How does the gospel compel you to love those who normally don't get a lot of love in society?

- **Observation:** What is the passage saying?
- **Application:** Where is Jesus asking me to repent?
- **Prayer:** How am I asking for enabling grace to repent?

DAY 20

READ:
Ecclesiastes 5:10-17; Proverbs 30:7-9; 1 Timothy 6:6-10

GREED

"Happiness comes when we recognize that all we possess belongs to God, because it comes from God. He even gives us the life in which we can possess things."

— Jim Winter, Ecclesiastes scholar and commentator

Here Solomon warns against the *love* of money and the delusions that wealth can bring. In Proverbs, Solomon advocates neither poverty nor riches, because both have their problems and temptations. Loving wealth and seeking for more never delivers the satisfaction that it promises. Ultimate peace of mind and security cannot be bought; they can only be received as gifts from God.

Where are you looking for money to provide what only God can? Where do you see examples of greed and materialism – i,e, wanting more – in your life? What drives your greed and materialism? Are you looking for comfort, status, security or some combination of these? How can the gospel provide you with these things fully so you can be set free from the love of money?

- **Observation:** What is the passage saying?
- **Application:** Where is Jesus asking me to repent?
- **Prayer:** How am I asking for enabling grace to repent?

DAY 21

READ:
Ecclesiastes 5:18-20; Philippians 4:11-13 ; Hebrews 13:5

ENJOYING TODAY

"The purpose of life is to live it, to taste experience to the utmost, to reach out eagerly and without fear for newer and richer experience."
– Eleanor Roosevelt

"If there lurks in most modern minds the notion that to desire our own good and to earnestly hope for the enjoyment of it is a bad thing, I suggest that this notion has crept in from Kant and the Stoics and is no part of the Christian faith."
– C.S. Lewis, author

Solomon returns to his frequent theme[2] of encouraging us to rest in and enjoy the gifts that God lavishes on us. Specifically, he recommends being very present in accepting where God has us now as protection from being lost in pining over the past.

Three weeks into this study, is Solomon's encouragement having any effect on you? Do you sense an underlying gratitude growing in your soul for God's goodness and grace? Do you ever find yourself thinking back on days gone by or looking forward to a day in the future? When we live presently we begin to see God moving around us. Pray the Lord would cause you to be so satisfied in Him that you are presently active.

- **Observation:** What is the passage saying?
- **Application:** Where is Jesus asking me to repent?
- **Prayer:** How am I asking for enabling grace to repent?

---

2 Ecclesiastes 2:24-25, 3:12-13

DAY 22

READ:
Ecclesiastes 6:1-6; Proverbs 19:23; Luke 18:18-30

LOOKING FOR SATISFACTION

"I can't get no satisfaction."

— The Rolling Stones

"I still haven't found what I'm looking for."

— Bono, U2

Once again Solomon brings a dramatic statement when he states that if a man has all kinds of good things in life but can't find satisfaction in them it'd be better to have never been born at all.

In Luke 18, Jesus meets a man similar to the one Solomon describes in Ecclesiastes 6:1-2. This man is rich, powerful, and a morally great fellow. But still he's unsatisfied and asks Jesus how to find eternal life.

Have you ever known anyone who seems to have it all, but still seems empty and unable to truly enjoy their life? Does that description describe you? Why does Jesus tell the rich man to sell all he has and give it to the poor? Why does the man walk away sad? Why does Jesus say, "How difficult it is for those who have wealth to enter the kingdom of God!"? Do you see a temptation for your soul to get numb toward Jesus in times when you have more wealth, comfort, and material possessions?

- **Observation:** What is the passage saying?
- **Application:** Where is Jesus asking me to repent?
- **Prayer:** How am I asking for enabling grace to repent?

DAY 23

READ:
Ecclesiastes 6:7-9; John 6:30-35 and 48-58; Philippians 3:18-20

ETERNAL APPETITES

"Sinful and forbidden pleasures are like poisoned bread; they may satisfy appetite for the moment, but there is death in them at the end."
— Tryon Edwards, American theologian

Solomon turns his view to our physical appetite as a metaphor for our spiritual longing and expresses the meaningless of appetite the same way he explained the boring repetition of nature in Chapter 1. No matter how many times we eat, we are never satisfied. In our fallen condition, we are perpetually hungry. This motif shows up throughout the Scriptures.[3] In John 6, Jesus makes some startling statements about our spiritual hunger when he tells a group of Jews that unless they eat his flesh, they will never be satisfied. Jesus is stating that there is no true satisfaction and life found outside of Him and His body sacrificed for us on the cross (v. 53).

Pick one meal this week to fast from food and just hang out with Jesus. What do you notice about yourself as you become more and more physically hungry? How is this a picture of our need for satisfaction in Jesus? Why does Jesus compare our need to Him to our need for food?

- **Observation:** What is the passage saying?
- **Application:** Where is Jesus asking me to repent?
- **Prayer:** How am I asking for enabling grace to repent?

---

[3] A few examples are: In Genesis 3, Satan tempts Eve with food and by telling her that God's boundaries on her life are limiting her search for fullness and satisfaction. In Exodus 16, God provides manna from heaven to ease the Israelites physical hunger, but also as a picture their spiritual need for His provision. In Matthew 26, Mark 14, Luke 22 and John 13, Jesus institutes communion as a picture of our need for Him.

DAY 24

READ:
Ecclesiastes 6:10-12; Genesis 32:24-30; Proverbs 3:5-6

SUBMITTING TO ONE STRONGER THAN US

"The reality of this world is that I was born into Someone Else's kingdom. My life came to me as a gift I did not choose; it is suspended from a slender thread that I did not weave and cannot on my own sustain. So I will need to… surrender. I crown another to be Master, Lord of my life. I offer my gifts, energies, resources, and heart to Him."

– John Ortberg

In Ecclesiastes 6:12, Solomon humbles his audience by reminding us that as hard as we try, we often have no idea what is good for our lives. In order to find the good life, we must submit our desires and our control to God who is stronger than us.

Towards the end of Jacob's story, there is a bizarre moment where he wrestles with God. Having searched for satisfaction in family, women, and hard work, Jacob realizes that God alone can satisfy his soul. So he clings onto God and says, "I will not let you go unless you bless me." In other words— "I'm done looking to other places for blessing. Only you can satisfy. I'm hanging on for dear life."

Where do you need to cling to God and refuse to keep searching for satisfaction in places that don't satisfy? What does it look like for you to surrender control of your desires to God's control and what He desires for your life?

- **Observation:** What is the passage saying?
- **Application:** Where is Jesus asking me to repent?
- **Prayer:** How am I asking for enabling grace to repent?

DAY 25

READ:
Ecclesiastes 7:1-14; 1 Corinthians 1:26-31; Ephesians 5:15-17

JESUS BECAME WISDOM TO US

"Wisdom begins in wonder."

– Socrates

"The fear of the Lord is the beginning of wisdom; fools despise wisdom and instruction."

– King Solomon in Proverbs 1:7

Throughout this section, Solomon offers us many proverbs – short wisdom sayings – that all have a unique Ecclesiastes flair. The first six verses encourage us to consider the benefits of things we normally try to avoid: sorrow, mourning, death and rebuke. The others are random statement as if you were getting coffee with your elderly grandpa. Sometimes you don't know what he's saying or why, but you also know he's forgotten more wisdom then you have yet learned.

As you read, which of these proverbs stand out to you and offer you insight into your life right now? What does 1 Corinthians 1:30 mean when it says Jesus became wisdom to us? How does the gospel enable and encourage us to apply Paul's seemingly impossible instructions in Ephesians 5:15-17?

- **Observation:** What is the passage saying?
- **Application:** Where is Jesus asking me to repent?
- **Prayer:** How am I asking for enabling grace to repent?

DAY 26

READ:
Ecclesiastes 7:15-20; Luke 18:9-14; Mark 2:15-17

WHIMSICAL HOLINESS

"Whimsical holiness is the ability to hold to personal values of Christ-likeness while being deeply integrated in relationship with people who do not hold your same convictions...Evangelicals often communicate a theology and practice of holiness based on avoidance of the world and worldly people. Jesus however, gave us a picture of holiness that included hanging out with worldly people."

– Hugh Halter, pastor and author

In this passage, Solomon proposes a funny sounding idea that it is both possible to be overly wicked and it is possible to be overly righteous. As funny as it sounds, it is deeply insightful as the Scriptures repetitively warn us that God despises a proud religious sense of self-righteousness. At the end of the day, the overly righteous trust in their own ability to be righteous and fail to see their desperate need for Jesus. As a result they often separate themselves from sinners in an attempt to achieve holiness by proximity. Jesus destroyed this mentality in the model of His ministry.

Are there any areas in your life where you are trusting in your religious works instead of Jesus' righteousness given to you as a gift? What kind of people are you unwilling to hang out with because they are too sinful and make you uncomfortable? Where is Jesus asking you to walk in whimsical holiness and engage those who are far from Him with His love?

- **Observation:** What is the passage saying?
- **Application:** Where is Jesus asking me to repent?
- **Prayer:** How am I asking for enabling grace to repent?

DAY 27

READ:
Ecclesiastes 7:21-29; Romans 3:11-12; 2 Corinthians 5:21

COMING TO GRIPS WITH OUR SPIRITUAL POVERTY

"The surest sign that we have received a spiritual understanding of God's love for us is the appreciation of our own poverty in light of His infinite mercy."

– Thomas Merton

"We were made for more than we can now have or even have the capacity to have in our fallen nature. We were made for unblemished intimacy and gourmet ecstasy. But we settle for crumbs. We settle for less because we're bored by waiting and discontent by our lot. Boredom says, 'I'm unable to enjoy myself.' Discontentment says, 'I should have become someone else by this point in my life.'"

– Abbie Smith, author of *Celibate Sex*

Solomon was a privileged king. He met prominent people from several different nations, yet he claimed, *"this alone I found, that God made man upright, but they have sought out many schemes."* (v. 29) If we don't understand the depth of our depravity, we won't cherish the abundant grace and forgiveness Jesus extends.

Where are you growingly aware of your spiritual poverty? How do you actively reflect on the fact that Jesus became sin for you so you could become His righteousness? What sin specifically did Jesus become for you?

- **Observation:** What is the passage saying?
- **Application:** Where is Jesus asking me to repent?
- **Prayer:** How am I asking for enabling grace to repent?

DAY 28

READ:
Ecclesiastes 8:1-9; Matthew 22:15-22; Romans 13:1-7

OBEY?

"There is no necessity to separate the monarch from the mob; all authority is equally bad."

– Oscar Wilde, Irish poet, playwright and author

"The modern world detests authority but worships relevance. Our Christian conviction is that the Bible has both authority and relevance, and that the secret of both is Jesus Christ."

– John Stott, theologian and author

Solomon states, *"I say: Keep the king's command, because of your oath to God."* (v. 2) Authority in our lives has a wide scope from parents when we are young, to teachers in school, to bosses at work, to pastors at church, and government throughout all our days.

Who in your life is the most difficult authority to submit to? Why? What does it look like to trust God as you submit to authority? How does Jesus both affirm authority and undermine authority at the same time in Matthew 22? What does it look like to submit to authorities while ultimately submitting to God's supreme authority?

- **Observation:** What is the passage saying?
- **Application:** Where is Jesus asking me to repent?
- **Prayer:** How am I asking for enabling grace to repent?

DAY 29

READ:
Ecclesiastes 8:10-13; Psalm 103:10-18; 2 Corinthians 6:16-7:1

FEARING GOD

"All understandings of all things that do not take God into consideration are superficial understandings, since they do not reckon with the true deepest connections with all things with what really matters in the universe, namely God. We today in America can scarcely begin to feel how God-ignoring we have become because it is the very air we breathe. We breathe God-ignoring air."

– John Piper, pastor and author

Solomon says the good life, where true contentment is found, is reserved for the person who fears God and lives reverently in his presence. In Psalm 103, David writes that God loves those who fear Him and *"does not deal with us according to our sin"* (v. 10).

What does it mean to fear God? Do you agree that in our culture we breathe God-ignoring air? How does fearing God cause us to hate sin and pursue holiness, while also causing us to doubt our righteousness and trust more and more in God's grace and forgiveness? Is there anywhere you are refusing to fear God and are trying to hide your sin from Him?

- **Observation:** What is the passage saying?
- **Application:** Where is Jesus asking me to repent?
- **Prayer:** How am I asking for enabling grace to repent?

DAY 30

READ:
Ecclesiastes 8:14-15; Romans 8:31-32; James 1:17

ENJOY!
"I can't ruin God's plan by asking or acting outside of it, but I can sleep through it. Forgetting that staying awake to God means staying awake to an abundance beyond my wildest creativity."

–Abbie Smith, author of Celibate Sex

Many Christians struggle with the concept of receiving gifts from God because they feel so undeserving and unworthy of enjoying His gifts. Some even tend to think that if they enjoy things, they are being selfish.

Solomon challenges this mentality stating repetitively that it is possible to enjoy God and the gifts He gives without feeling guilty. Specifically here he notes that our righteousness nor our wickedness determines how the circumstances of our life will necessarily go,; so enjoy what you've got now while you have it.

Do you tend to feel guilty about enjoying God's good gifts? Do you lean more toward over-indulgence, or over-restriction? Why? How in Jesus can you be freed up to receive everything as a gift from a loving Father? How in Jesus can you repent from enjoying the gifts but missing out on God?

- **Observation:** What is the passage saying?
- **Application:** Where is Jesus asking me to repent?
- **Prayer:** How am I asking for enabling grace to repent?

DAY 31

READ:
Ecclesiastes 8:16-17; Psalm 139:1-18; Matthew 10:29-31

GOD WHO KNOWS AND CONTROLS EVERYTHING

"To say that God is omniscient is to say that He possesses perfect knowledge and therefore has no need to learn. But it is more: it is to say that God has never learned and cannot learn."

- A.W. Tozer, *The Knowledge of the Holy*

"I believe God is managing affairs and that He doesn't need any advice from me. With God in charge, I believe everything will work out for the best in the end. So what is there to worry about?"

– Henry Ford, Founder of Ford Motor Company

Solomon reflects on his pursuit of wisdom and compares his tiny understanding to God who knows and controls everything. No matter how hard we search; we will never fully understand everything God is actively causing to work under the sun.

And in the midst of knowing and controlling everything in the universe, King David writes that God intimately knows you and me. Have you ever pondered God's omniscience? What feelings arise as you think about God's intricate knowledge of your every detail?

- **Observation:** What is the passage saying?
- **Application:** Where is Jesus asking me to repent?
- **Prayer:** How am I asking for enabling grace to repent?

DAY 32

READ:
Ecclesiastes 9:1-3; Romans 5:12-18; Revelation 21:2-4

UNNATURAL DEATH

"Death is the great obscenity of our age. Men and women will air their sex lives and other intimate details on television talk shows, but they will not talk about death… The Bible, on the other hand, speaks openly and often about death. According to the Bible, we fear death because it is unnatural. God made man in His image and gave him an immortal soul. Man wants to live forever, but death abruptly terminates his conscious physical existence."

– Dr. Joseph A. Pipa, a member of Ligonier Ministries

As Solomon turns his gaze to death under the sun once again, he despairs the reality that death comes for us all, regardless of who we are. Instead of just observing this fact, Solomon bemoans it: *"This is an evil in all that is done under the sun, that the same event happens to all."* He bemoans the fact because he's realizing what the Scriptures say over and over: death is unnatural. Romans 5 states that death did not enter the world until sin did.

What role has death played in your life? Have you lost any friends or family members unexpectedly or in a tragic way? Can you imagine what the world will be like when God removes death?

- **Observation:** What is the passage saying?
- **Application:** Where is Jesus asking me to repent?
- **Prayer:** How am I asking for enabling grace to repent?

DAY 33

READ:
Ecclesiastes 9:4-9; John 8:31-36; Galatians 5:1; 1 Peter 2:16

FREEDOM THROUGH CHRIST

"May we think of freedom, not as the right to do as we please, but as the opportunity to do what is right."

– Peter Marshall

Look closely at Verse 7 in this section of Ecclesiastes: *"Go, eat your bread with joy, and drink your wine with a merry heart, for God has already approved what you do."*

Here we get a glimpse in the Old Testament of the freedom we experience in the New Testament through Jesus Christ. At this time, Solomon had the promise of Jesus' coming, but did not have Jesus Himself yet. When we accept God's forgiveness through Jesus we are able to enjoy the freedom Solomon could only see in a shadow.

Are there any areas of life where you would say you are not currently experiencing the freedom of Christ? How can you press into the gospel and allow Jesus' grace to lead you into deeper and deeper freedom?

- **Observation:** What is the passage saying?
- **Application:** Where is Jesus asking me to repent?
- **Prayer:** How am I asking for enabling grace to repent?

DAY 34

READ:
Ecclesiastes 9:10; 1 Corinthians 10:23-33; 1 John 3:16-18

LOVING IN DEED AND TRUTH

"One good deed is more worth than a thousand brilliant theories."
— Charles Spurgeon, pastor and author.

"There are risks and costs to action. But they are far less than the long range risks of comfortable inaction."
— John F. Kennedy, President of the United States.

Solomon begs us to act with all of our might while we can act and before we find ourselves in the grave. John begs with us to love in deed and truth and not just in word. Paul argues that he would be willing to do anything – enjoying his freedom or denying his freedom – if that will potentially lead to many being saved.

Have you ever had a great idea but failed to follow through with it? How can you put into action today one thing that the Lord has put on your heart to do? How can you build a system to ensure more of your ideas become reality in the future?

- **Observation:** What is the passage saying?
- **Application:** Where is Jesus asking me to repent?
- **Prayer:** How am I asking for enabling grace to repent?

DAY 35

READ:
Ecclesiastes 9:11-18; 1 Corinthians 9:24-27; Hebrews 12:1-2

FAITHFUL MOTIVATION FOR THE LONG HAUL

"In NASCAR, you don't have to be as physically strong as in some other forms of racing. You've just got to be able to endure the heat and endurance of it."

— Jeff Gordon, NASCAR Race Driver.

Solomon observes that time and chance mean the people you expect to win aren't always those who win. *"The race is not to the swift."* (v. 11) In light of the fact that death comes for all of us and we don't know when it's going to come, the only option is to run faithfully the race marked out for us with endurance.

Solomon moves on to a story of a poor man whose advice saved his city. Unfortunately, he doesn't get the credit for it and everyone forgets about him. He faithfully runs his race and rescues many people's lives but doesn't get earthly recognition.

What motivates you to run the race faithfully that Jesus has laid out for you? If you would never get any credit or recognition, would you still be willing to do whatever Jesus calls you to do?

- **Observation:** What is the passage saying?
- **Application:** Where is Jesus asking me to repent?
- **Prayer:** How am I asking for enabling grace to repent?

DAY 36

READ:
Ecclesiastes 10:1-7; Psalm 1; Matthew 7:24-29

PUFFED UP WITH KNOWLEDGE

"Wisdom is the right use of knowledge. To know is to be wise. Many men know a great deal, and are all the greater fools for it. There is no great a fool as a knowing fool. But to know how to use knowledge is to have wisdom."

– Charles Spurgeon, pastor and author

Solomon drops several wisdom teachings that help differentiate the wise man from the foolish man. It is not simply how much knowledge *about* God we have that measures wisdom, but how we *apply* what we know about God in our lives. Jesus often preached to the "foolish" of the world (the lowly, uneducated, sinners, tax collectors) and spoke of the impending doom coming to the "wise" (educated, Pharisees, self-righteous).

Why do you think Jesus chose the foolish of the world to be the ones to understand and receive His spiritual truths? What are your motives are for wanting to gain wisdom? Are you being a good steward of the knowledge God has already given to you about himself? Mediate on 1 Corinthians 8:1, "Knowledge makes arrogant, but love edifies."

- **Observation:** What is the passage saying?
- **Application:** Where is Jesus asking me to repent?
- **Prayer:** How am I asking for enabling grace to repent?

DAY 37

READ:
Ecclesiastes 10:8-20; James 3:6; Proverbs 10:19; Ephesians 4:25-26 and 29-32

IDLE CHATTER

"Whatever the topic of conversation, the spirit of piety should be diffused through it—as the salt in our food should properly season it all, whatever the article of food may be."

–Albert Barnes, writer and educator

In verses 12-15, Solomon teaches that wisdom is learning how to govern and tame our tongues. The Bible lists many sins that are sins of the tongue including malicious gossip about others, complaining about circumstances, being divisive, or trying to impress friends with lies and exaggerated stories. Solomon says fools talk a lot with little aim or purpose in their speech. The words of a fool expose his foolishness. In contrast, a wise man's words are gracious, good, and edifying to those who hear them.

As you go through the day, listen to what you're saying. Do you find yourself mindlessly chatting about nothing? How can you grow in considering what purposes God has for your words when you choose to speak?

- **Observation:** What is the passage saying?
- **Application:** Where is Jesus asking me to repent?
- **Prayer:** How am I asking for enabling grace to repent?

DAY 38

READ:
Ecclesiastes 11:1-6; Deuteronomy 29:29; Ephesians 3:8-10

THE MYSTERIES OF GOD

"When we understand the outside of things, we think we have them. Yet the Lord puts his things in subdefined, suggestive shapes, yielding no satisfactory meaning to the mere intellect, but unfolding themselves to the conscience of the heart."

– George Macdonald, author, poet and Christian minister

Solomon starts this passage by encouraging wise investments and hard diligent work in light of the fact that we do not know how things will play out. He actually encourages foreign investments and a diversified portfolio. Then in v. 5 he states, *"As you do not know the way the spirit comes to the bones in the womb of a woman with child, so you do not know the work of God who makes everything."*

God is bigger than us and therefore we cannot fathom all of his thoughts. If we could understand everything He knows and does, then He would cease to be a God worthy of our worship. If God told us everything He knew, we would have no need for dependence, humility or faith.

Are there any areas of life where you are frustrated with God or wanting more clarity? How might God be using this frustration to grow your faith?

- **Observation:** What is the passage saying?
- **Application:** Where is Jesus asking me to repent?
- **Prayer:** How am I asking for enabling grace to repent?

DAY 39

READ:
Ecclesiastes 11:6 – 12:8; Job 14:1-2; Mark 10:13-16

REMEMBERING (IN) OUR YOUTH

"Good habits formed at youth make all the difference."

– Aristotle

"Youth is happy because it has the ability to see beauty. Anyone who keeps the ability to see beauty never grows old."

– Franz Kafka

Solomon is not inviting us to chase after our fleeting pleasures and idols, but to live joyfully in the world God created and rules over. He pleads with readers, "Don't procrastinate when it comes to following God. When all the enjoyments of life turn sour, when death strikes, when you lose your job and feel defeated, remember all that God has done for you in the past. Remember before you lose your perception and things grow overwhelming. Remember His goodness, His kind pursuit of you, His calling. Remember He is in control. Remember God before you lose your strength, drive, and stamina. Give God all you have now. It's not too late.

Take some time to mediate on what God has done for you, how He's proven Himself faithful and trustworthy. Where would you be without God's grace at work in your life? What are pivotal moments in your life when God has shown up?

- **Observation:** What is the passage saying?
- **Application:** Where is Jesus asking me to repent?
- **Prayer:** How am I asking for enabling grace to repent?

DAY 40

READ:
Ecclesiastes 12:9-14; John 14:23-24 and 15:12-14; 2 John 1:6

LAST WORDS
"Faith [is] a living flaming thing leading to surrender and obedience to the commandments of Christ."
— A.W. Tozer, pastor and author

"Few of us know what it's like to be unburdened by fear. We imagine it would make us bolder and braver. In reality, it would make us stupider. Fear, as it turns out, is a fundamental part of making good decisions."
— Kelly McGonigal, Stanford Ph.D. health psychologist

Solomon ends the book with a weighty summary: *"Fear God and keep his commandments, for this is the whole duty of man. For God will bring every deed into judgment, with every secret thing, whether good or evil."* Solomon sums up his entire book about the meaning of life and concludes all of his thoughts in one statement, "Fear God and obey Him."

How does obeying God lead to the good life? When God asks you to obey him, what is your range of internal and external response? Are there any areas where you've been ignoring God instead of fearing Him? Do you need to confess and repent?

- **Observation:** What is the passage saying?
- **Application:** Where is Jesus asking me to repent?
- **Prayer:** How am I asking for enabling grace to repent?

SECTION THREE
FAMILY GUIDE

INTRODUCTION

A quick drive up I-26 in the fall and you'll notice the leaves changing. Trees on the banks of our three rivers will explode with orange, yellow, red, and brown. In Columbia, the fall is a great chance to play with your children outside without drowning in sweat. For many of you, the fall also brings the busy hum of a rapid pace of life. After starting with the excitement and anxiety of a new school year, most of us settle into a rhythm of school, extracurricular activities, and trying to catch a college football game or two on the weekends.

Fall tends to be an event-heavy season. From PTO meetings to holiday dinners, the sheer volume of events can become stressful for many families. As you lead your family through seasons like the fall we want to help you point your kids towards Christ in the midst of the chaos. The Family Activity Guide is designed to help you be intentional with the time you spend together.

There is a charge given in the book of Deuteronomy to continually and intentionally talk with children about what it means to love God with all they are – no matter where they are, no matter what they're doing:

> "Hear, O Israel: The Lord our God, the Lord, is one. You shall love the Lord your God with all your heart and with all your soul and with all your might. And these words that I command you today shall be on your heart. You shall teach them diligently to your children, and shall talk of them when you sit in your house, and

> *when you walk by the way, and when you lie down, and when you rise. You shall bind them as a sign on your hand, and they shall be as frontlets between your eyes. You shall write them on the doorposts of your house and on your gates."*

Deuteronomy 6:4-9

This charge was in mind when putting together this activity guide. Whether you're hanging out at home, traveling to Grandma's for Thanksgiving, or running errands around town, there is no shortage of opportunities to help your children see Jesus at work in your life and in their lives. We are praying that you will see and take advantage of these moments.

HOW TO BEST USE THE ACTIVITY GUIDE

This guide is designed to be a helpful resource for your family as you think about—and plan— what your fall will look like. Most of these activities and devotionals have been written with elementary-age children in mind. Many of them can be modified for younger or older children, or for families with children across a broad age range. For little babies and toddlers we've also included Prayer Guides. Here are a few tips on how to get the most out of this activity guide:

DON'T TRY IT ALL

The goal here is not to make you busier, but to help you build your family with Jesus at the center. This activity guide contains more things than your family will probably be able to do. So don't try to do it all. Pick what will be most helpful for you to lead your family. Let this be a blessing to your family and not a religious burden.

PLAN AHEAD
No one stumbles into intentionality. Take time to think and pray about what you want this fall to be like for your family. At the end of it, what do you want your kids to remember? How do you want them to have grown? What do you hope they learn about Jesus? What will you put in place to help make that happen?

HAVE FUN!
No matter what your family plans are for this season – make sure you have fun! Enjoy being with your kids. Laugh a lot. Make memories out of every moment – even the most mundane ones.

USE A KID-FRIENDLY TRANSLATION OF THE BIBLE
For Kidtown, we use the New International Reader's Version. It's a fairly accurate, simplified translation to help your children understand what they are reading.

KEEP IT HANDY
You never know when you will be stuck in traffic and end up with 20 minutes that could be perfect for one of these activities or devotionals. In light of Deuteronomy's charge to teach God's truth "diligently to your children", keep a copy of this activity guide handy so you can intentionally turn these opportunities into Jesus moments.

DO IT WITH YOUR LIFEGROUP
Too often we keep parenting and family life secluded from our shared life with our LifeGroup. Many of these activities and devotionals in this activity guide offer a great opportunity to share life together with other people and families in our LifeGroup. Invite single people (and couples with no kids) to come get a view and play a pivotal role in your family. Invite other families and their kids to participate in the devotionals with you. Make it a fun date

night where you do the devotional this week and watch some other people's kids. Next week they can watch your kids and lead the devotional.

FAMILY ACTIVITIES

SEEKING REFUGE

Like the book of Ecclesiastes we are studying, Psalms is another book that is full of these types of wisdom writings. Here is an activity you can do with your children that will create fun memories, and give you an opportunity to unpack some wisdom from the Psalms with them.

After dinner one night, build a fort (probably in the living room) your family will camp out in for the night. Use blankets, pillows, furniture, lamps, flashlights, and duct tape – whatever makes it fun and exciting for your kids. As you build the fort, talk about the purposes of a fort with your children. Why do people build forts (protection, safety, shelter, etc.)? Then, while you're in the fort before bed, talk about the refuge we can find in God. Read Psalm 144:1-2:

> *"Give praise to the Lord. He is my rock. He trains my hands for war. He trains my fingers for battle. He is my loving God. He is like a fort to me. He is my place of safety and the One who saves me. He is like a shield that keeps me safe. I go to him for safety. He brings nations under my control."*

Ask them some of the following questions and keep pointing them towards the reality that when they are going through bad days, they can get "into the fort with God" and take refuge in Him:

- Are there any words in these verses you do not recognize or understand?
- Whom is David, the writer of this Psalm, talking about?
- What things does David compare God to?
- What do these things (a rock, fortress, stronghold, deliverer, refuge and shield) have in common? How would you describe them?

Tell them about some times in your life when Jesus has provided refuge for you. Praise God for being a refuge for His children. Ask Him for faith to trust in His protection in hard and scary times.

HAVE A MEAL WITH YOUR CHILD'S KIDTOWN LEADER

You may or may not have heard a lot about your child's Kidtown leaders, but these faithful volunteers lovingly care for your child week after week. This activity will help you teach your kids about hospitality and show our volunteers they are appreciated. After talking to your kids, pick a Kidtown leader or two to invite over for dinner one night. Make an invitation with your kids and give it to their Kidtown leader one week after the Gathering.

Before they come over, read Romans 12:13 with your kids:

> *"Share with God's people who are in need. Welcome others into your homes."*

Talk to your kids about offering hospitality to church family and respecting authority. Help them understand why God gives us good authority figures as a blessing. Have your kids write a thank you letter to their Kidtown leader and give it to them at dinner. Give your child opportunities to help set the table, prepare and serve the food, and clean up at the end.

FALL MEMORY JAR

The book of Ecclesiastes stresses the importance of acknowledging and remembering what God has done for us while we are young:

> "Remember your Creator in the days of your youth, before the days of trouble come and the years approach when you will say, 'I find no pleasure in them.'"

> –Ecclesiastes 12:1

To practically apply this idea, throughout the fall keep track of good memories and spiritual lessons learned in a Fall Memory Jar. For this activity, put a jar or container in a central location within your house. Label it "Fall Memory Jar" and put small strips of paper next to it. When a memorable moment or lesson happens, your kids can go to the jar, write down the memory and place it inside. Give them the freedom to put what they want inside the jar – you may be surprised with what they consider a memory!

Go through the memories in the jar on a weekly basis. Dump out the contents of the jar and go back through the jar. Thank God together for the great times and lessons learned throughout this season. This is a great rhythm to join up with a few families in your LifeGroup. Occasionally get together as families and share with each other the jar memories.

POPSICLE PRAYERS

In Matthew 28, Jesus gives us an invitation to be part of His mission to share the gospel with those around us. In 1st Timothy 2:1, Paul encourages us to pray for all kinds of people in all kinds of ways. As a church family, we are called to consistently pray for our city, and our neighbors— that they may might come to know Jesus and His grace.

As a family, spend time praying for your friends this fall. Let your children pick some of their friends to pray for and you can add some of your friends, co-workers, or neighbors. Write each person's name on a Popsicle stick and put all the sticks in any kind of can or container. Set a time during the week to pray for your friends, drawing two or three sticks out of the can.

Whenever you see Jesus actively working in any of these people's lives, make sure you point it out to your kids. Thank Jesus for how He answers prayer and how He invites us to be a part of what He's doing in people's lives.

DAILY CARE CALLS

This family activity is a simple way to grow in expressing love for church family and others. Pick a regular time of day – it could be every night after you read a bible story together or every day on the way home from school – to call one person and ask how they are doing. Let them know you love them and ask how you can pray for them. These phone calls can provide people and specific things to add to your popsicle prayers if you choose to participate in that activity.

A PLACE AND TIME TO FOCUS

While children are often full of unfocused energy, part of the job of parenting is coaching them in how to calm down, be quiet, and focus. From spiritual to practical implications, studies show that children who develop self-control at a young age experience blessings throughout their life.[1]

To help with self-control, focus, thinking, prayer, and studying the Bible, set up a family plan for how you will all have a place and time to focus. This will look different for children of different ages and reading levels. A first grader's place and time might be: "read and pray with Mom or Dad for 15 minutes on the couch after dinner". For a fifth grader, an appropriate time and place might be: "Read the Bible and pray for 30 minutes in my room before bed".

As your children are able, encourage them to journal (or write out prayers) and set aside some time to talk about what you are thinking about, praying about and learning in your place and time to focus. [2]

GET TO KNOW YOUR NEIGHBORS

Often, parks and libraries serve as neighborhood Gathering places where kids go to play or read with their parents. Use these neighborhood hangouts as an opportunity to meet and talk with your neighbors. Invite other LifeGroup families to come with you to the park and you can meet these neighbors together.

Set the goal that as a family you're going to befriend one new family throughout the fall and try to get to know them. Here are some options: You could invite them over for dinner. You could invite them over to play. You could invite them over to watch a football game.

Before or after having them over, read the following scriptures as a family and talk about God's purpose for you in your neighborhood and community: Matthew 28:18-20; Acts 17:24-27. You can

---

[1] Go to www.midtowncolumbia.com/GoodLifeLinks Section 3: Link #1 for more creative leaf art for kids' ideas.
[2] Section 2 of this book – the Good Life personal devotional and reading plan – can be a helpful resource for your study as well as what you're reading and praying through as a family.

also add their names to your Popsicle prayer jar if you've got one or this could be a good way to start one.

SEEING JESUS IN THE LEAVES:

At some point during the fall, go for a nature walk with your family. If you've got the time, you can drive up to the mountains where the changing leaves are absolutely beautiful. Ask your kids simple questions like: What do you like about the colorful trees? Which one is your favorite color? Why do the leaves change colors? The changing leaves of fall are a great chance to emphasize multiple spiritual truths:

1. Seasons – Solomon describes many different seasons in Ecclesiastes. *"There is a time for everything, and a season for every activity under the heavens"* (3:1). This is a great time to talk about God's control of the "seasons" of our lives with our kids. Most children don't have a huge understanding of seasons in life, but they can understand good and bad days. Use the fall as an opportunity to teach them that God has a purpose for the good and bad days. He wants to teach us about His goodness even when life is hard.

2. Beauty – The amazing canvas of leaves changing color are a great chance to talk about God's love of beauty and His artistic nature seen throughout creation. Help your kids connect that all their favorite things in life (including colors, nature, trees, leaves, toys, family, hugs, stuffed animals, etc) are all good gifts from our loving Father in heaven. Reference Matthew 7:7-11 and James 1:17.

3. Change – Leaves changing color is a great opportunity to talk to kids about the reality that things change in life. Our relationships change. Our grades and subjects in school change. How does change make them feel? Do they like change or not like change? Tell them how change makes you feel. Do you like it or not? When we don't like change, how can we help encourage each other and support each other? In some ways, God is the only thing in the world that doesn't change. Reference Hebrews 13:8 and Psalm 102:25-27.

CREATE YOUR OWN ART EXHIBIT

God is incredibly creative. You can see this in the variety of colors, textures, shapes and sounds that are present in creation. Being creative is one of the ways people reflect the image of God.

For this family activity, express your creativity by making your own art exhibit. Collect some leaves and use them for various art projects (leaf rubbing, sketches, collages, etc.)[3] Look for things you already have around the house that can be transformed into art – dried pasta, cereal, newspaper, paper towel tubes, yarn, empty jars – along with normal art supplies. Use these materials to create works of art. Name each piece and hang them in your home, creating your own art installation. Read Genesis 1 with your kids (in a kid-friendly translation) and talk about how God created the world with so much beauty and creativity and how He created us in His image.

---

3 Go to www.midtowncolumbia.com/GoodLifeLinks Section 3: Link #3 for more creative leaf art for kids' ideas.

FAMILY DEVOTIONALS

WEEK 1: THE TREADMILL
Here on earth, life can be filled with some repetitive cycles. These boring, repetitious cycles reveal to us that nothing in the world really makes us happy deep down in our hearts. We need Jesus to really make us happy deep down in our hearts. Without Jesus we miss out on the real point of life!

REVIEW
On the ride home from the Gathering, ask your child questions 1-4 listed below. These questions are the same every week for two reasons:
- To help provide an anticipated rhythm for your family after a Gathering.
- To reinforce Kidtown's main points of emphasis - learning, fun, and relationships.
1. What did you learn today at Kidtown?
2. What was the most fun part of today?
3. Did you meet anyone new?
4. How can we pray for your friends at Kidtown this week?

DIG DEEPER
After dinner one evening, open the Bible and lead your kids in this devotional based on the Kidtown lesson.

1. Read Ecclesiastes 1:9-11 aloud as a family.
- Were there any words we just read that you didn't understand?
- This book was written by King Solomon, one of the wisest people to ever live.
- What do you think it would be like to be a king?

2. How does King Solomon describe life in this verse?
King Solomon has observed that life is very repetitive and routine like running on a treadmill. This exposes to him that nothing on earth truly satisfies our deepest questions and desires.

3. What is an example of something you have to do over and over in your life?
Prompt them with any of the following: Go to school every morning, brush your teeth every day, take out the trash, etc.

4. Does this ever get boring?
If they don't know what to say, tell them if the repetitive cycles of life every get boring for you.

5. How do think Jesus gives meaning to our lives?
This is a hard question for kids to answer, give them some time to think about it. Help them see that what Jesus does lasts forever. Jesus helps us view everyday routines as opportunities to love Him and other people.

PRAY TOGETHER AS A FAMILY
Thank you Jesus for allowing us to have lives that don't have to be boring. You give us purpose in all that we do.

MEMORY VERSE

"What has been is what will be, and what has been done is what will be done, and there is nothing new under the Sun."

- Ecclesiastes 1:9

INTERACTIVE FAMILY DEVOTIONAL

To help demonstrate we need Jesus to set us free from the boring, meaningless things we chase after for satisfaction on earth, set up a game of Jailbreak!

(If there aren't enough people in your family, grab some other families from your LifeGroup or from the neighborhood.) Jailbreak begins with children split into two teams. One team begins as the "cops" and the other as the "criminals." When a member of the cop team captures a criminal, he takes him to a designated area that is called "jail." A free member of the criminal team can free their teammate by tagging them and yelling "JAILBREAK!!." However, if the child trying to free his team members is caught, he must also go to jail. The teams switch roles when everyone on the criminal team has been captured and put into jail.

After the game, ask some questions about what it felt like to be stuck in jail and not able to get where you are trying to go? What did it feel like when they got set free from jail? Help explain to them that trying to find deep down happiness for our hearts on earth just gets us stuck in a jail we can't get out of. Jesus alone brings us real freedom and helps us experience His purpose in life. Reference Galatians 5:1.

WEEK 2: THE EXPERIMENT

King Solomon tests and experiments with every kind of happiness that people try out in life. After finishing his experiment, he realizes that nothing on earth can deliver on its promises. Over time, toys break, friends and siblings hurt our feelings, and nothing turns out to make us as happy deep down as we thought it would.

REVIEW
On your ride home from the Gathering, ask your child the following questions:
1. What did you learn today at Kidtown?
2. What was the most fun part of today?
3. Did you meet anyone new?
4. How can we pray for your friends at Kidtown this week?

DIG DEEPER
After dinner one evening, open the Bible and lead your kids in a devotional based on the Kidtown lesson.

1. Read Ecclesiastes 2:1-17 together as a family.
- Are there any words that you didn't understand in these verses?
- Was anything interesting to you in these verses?

2. What would help you to be the happiest person alive?
Solomon uses all of his wisdom to test all the things that people look to in order to be happy. Use this question to get to know your kids better and understand the things that they really think would make them happy deep down.

3. What does King Solomon say he did in this passage?
The world around King Solomon said that life would be best if we made life about having fun, getting rich, and being smart. So he got more stuff, more money, had more fun, and did more than almost any other human being in the history of the world.

4. What does he say he figured out about these things?
These things were like "striving after the wind". You can't catch the wind! They never delivered what he was looking for. You can't find ultimate satisfaction or meaning in pleasure, fun, being rich, or being smart. Living your life for these things will leave you feeling empty. A wise person will live for something beyond what is temporary.

QUICK INTERACTIVE

Tell your kids to go get a broken toy, or a toy they don't like that much anymore that was really, really fun when they first got it. Use this as an illustration to help them see that it was temporary and didn't deliver lasting happiness.

5. How do you think Jesus wants our family to live for more than our own fun, money, and comfort?
Help prompt your kids to think of practical ways that they can serve others and love Jesus.

PRAY TOGETHER AS A FAMILY

Thank God that He brings great meaning and purpose to our lives. Ask Him to help us see that He is more fulfilling than anything else we might think can make us happy.

MEMORY VERSE

> "What has been is what will be, and what has been done is what will be done, and there is nothing new under the Sun."
>
> - Ecclesiastes 1:9

INTERACTIVE FAMILY ACTIVITY

Solomon compares us trying to find satisfaction in things of this world to a "striving after the wind". To help our kids see what Solomon is trying to say, go into a room and put on some sort of fan. If you have a box fan, that will be perfect. Encourage your kids to try and catch the wind coming out of the fan. Put some fun music on and give them five minutes to try (This is also a great way to get energy out before bed!). Have a bucket on the side where they are supposed to put the wind they catch.

Encourage them to be creative in thinking up different ways to try to catch the wind. (pillow cases, plastic bags, etc.) In the end, no matter what they try, they will have no wind in their bucket. Help them see that their efforts to catch wind are ultimately useless. Use this to help you explain Solomon's perspective on everything he chased after in his life.

WEEK 3: THE TROPHY CLUB

Everybody wants to be successful in life. We want to get trophies. We want to be popular. We want to be smart. We want to be good looking. The danger is that we can start to believe that being successful is what makes us important. This is a silly trade for Jesus' love as our source of satisfaction and will never make us happy deep down.

REVIEW:

On your ride home from the Gathering, ask your child the following questions:
1. What did you learn today at Kidtown?
2. What was the most fun part of today?
3. Did you meet anyone new?
4. How can we pray for your friends at Kidtown this week?

DIG DEEPER:

After dinner one evening, open the Bible and lead your kids in a devotional based on the Kidtown lesson.

1. Read Ecclesiastes 2:18-20 together as a family.
Remind your family from last week how King Solomon had more money and accomplished more things than most any human being ever would. Ask your kids if there were any words that they didn't understand in these verses?

2. Do you ever feel like you have to do something to be valuable or for people to like you? If so, what is it?
Prompts here could include being obedient at school or at home. Follow up with questions like: Do you ever do things that make people mad at you? Do you ever do things that make you feel like people don't love you?

3. Does King Solomon think that being successful makes us valuable? Why not?

No. Surprisingly, Solomon says that even though we all want to win at life, being successful, smart, athletic, good looking, or popular don't actually bring lasting joy. It's fleeting pleasure that can't answer our deepest questions in life: Who am I? Am I significant? Am I loved? We can never have enough trophies or big enough trophies.

4. Read 2:24-25. What does King Solomon say that we should do?

Instead of finding our worth in what we accomplish, we can find our worth in Jesus loving us no matter what we do. Success in sports or school or popularity will never be able to give us meaning or worth like Jesus can. Feel free to give examples from your life where you thought a promotion or a certain successful project would bring you life but it failed to do so.

PRAY TOGETHER AS A FAMILY

Thank God for his good gifts of school, work, and fun. Ask Him to protect us from believing that being successful in these areas will give us meaning and worth. Ask Him to help us know that He gives us meaning and worth through Jesus.

MEMORY VERSE

> "I perceived that there is nothing better for them than to be joyful and to do good as long as they live."
>
> - Ecclesiastes 3:12

INTERACTIVE FAMILY ACTIVITY:

Get a packet of note cards. Ask your kids to give you 10 different professions, then write them down on the cards. To make this easier for them, ask them for their three favorite professions (i.e. What do you want to be when you grow up?). Then ask them for their three least favorite professions (i.e. What do you *definitely* not want to be when you grow up?). And finally ask them for some other professions they know of (potentially yours if it isn't already listed). When all ten are written down, have your kids rank the jobs from the most important job to the least (put them in order).

Read 1 Corinthians 10:31:

"Whatever you do, weather you eat or drink, do it all to the glory of God"

How can each of the jobs we listed be used for the glory of God? Ask your kids what are some pros and cons about each of these jobs? Why do we tend to think some jobs are more important than other ones? Help them to realize the value and importance of each of the professions. Share with them how Jesus loves people regardless of their work. Their worth is not in what they accomplish but in the way Jesus views them.

WEEK 4: THE ILLUSION OF CONTROL

Solomon was the smartest man who ever lived and he wrote a beautiful poem that describes lots of different seasons that happen during life. This poem helps us to see that we are not in control of what seasons of life we go through. God controls the seasons of life that we experience. Whether the seasons feel good or bad, God wants to use the season to love us and to help us grow.

REVIEW

On your ride home from the Gathering, ask your child the following questions:
1. What did you learn today at Kidtown?
2. What was the most fun part of today?
3. Did you meet anyone new?
4. How can we pray for your friends at Kidtown this week?

DIG DEEPER

After dinner one evening, open the Bible and lead your kids in a devotional based on the Kidtown lesson.

1. Read Ecclesiastes 3:1-8, 14 together as a family.
- Question: Are there any words that you don't understand in these verses?

2. Interactive Family Activity:
This week we're going to start with the interactive family activity. Ask your kids to go find four different things that represent each season within your house. Instruct them to pick one item for fall, winter, spring, and summer. Give them a certain amount of time to find these things (two minutes each) and have them bring them back to you.

Now it's time for show and tell! Have each child explain why they picked the things they picked to represent the different seasons of the year. This activity gives you a perfect segue to explain that there are lots of different seasons (good, bad, tough, fun, etc.) in our lives. Talk about Ecclesiastes 3:1 *"There is a time for everything, and a season for every activity under the heavens"*

3. Do you remember a time that you felt out of control?
Prompt: potential examples can include a time you got angry towards your sibling or if you've ever been afraid because you thought you got lost.

4. How did being out of control make you feel?
Ask them if they felt scared, uncertain, confused, afraid, etc.?

5. What are things you can control in your life? What are some things you can't control?
Help prompt and teach your kids that things we can control are our thoughts and feelings and our reactions to circumstances. What we can't control are the circumstances in our lives or how other people treat us.

6. What does Ecclesiastes 9:1 teach us?

> *"I realized that those who are wise and do what is right are under God's control. What they do is also under his control."*

God is always in control. He is in control of everything that happens in life. We don't have to be afraid when things seem out of control to us. God will take care of those who trust Him. That doesn't mean that things will always be easy, but it does mean God is still there.

8. How do you know we can trust God when things seem out of control?

We can trust God to care for us always because of Jesus. Jesus died for our sins on a cross. If He didn't abandon us in our sin then, we can be certain He won't abandon us in anything! Read Romans 8:31-35 as a family.

> "What should we say then? Since God is on our side, who can be against us? God did not spare his own Son. He gave him up for us all. Then won't He also freely give us everything else? Who can bring any charge against God's chosen ones? God makes us right with Himself. Who can sentence us to death? Christ Jesus is at the right hand of God and is also praying for us. He died. More than that, He was raised to life."

PRAY TOGETHER AS A FAMILY

Thank God that He is in control. Thank Him that we don't have to be in control because He is. Ask Him to help your family trust in Him. Ask Him to remind your family constantly of the work He did for us in Jesus and how that shows us we can trust Him even when we feel out of control.

MEMORY VERSE

> "I perceived that there is nothing better for them than to be joyful and to do good as long as they live."
>
> Ecclesiastes 3:12

Insight from Ecclesiastes

WEEK 5: FLYING SOLO

God designed us to live life together and to share life. Solomon explains that if you get hurt, cold, or lost, you need friends to help you out! But sometimes it's hard to get along with others! This week we will look at the wisdom Solomon gives us that we were meant to share life with others.

REVIEW

On your ride home from the Gathering, ask your child the following questions:
1. What did you learn today at Kidtown?
2. What was the most fun part of today?
3. Did you meet anyone new?
4. How can we pray for your friends at Kidtown this week?

DIG DEEPER

After dinner one evening, open the Bible and lead your kids in a devotional based on the Kidtown lesson.

1. Read Ecclesiastes 4:9-12 aloud together.
- Question: Are there any words that you don't understand in these verses?

2. What does it looks like to share life with your friends? Where do you see examples of people sharing life together (family, LifeGroup, school, etc)?
On sports teams you work together as a team. At school, you often have group projects where you work with your friends on something. Simply, sharing life together is choosing to help each other instead of trying to do life on our own.

3. Who do you think God has called us to share our lives with?

1.) *Our family.* He's given us each other. (Read Ephesians 2:19-20) 2.) *Our church family.* Believers in Jesus have been made a family, just like ours, through the sacrifice Jesus made for all of us. Our LifeGroup is an example of our church family. 3.) (Read 1 Peter 2:9) *Those who do not yet know Jesus.* God has given believers a purpose— to help those who don't know Him yet to get to know Him.

4. What makes sharing life with other people difficult sometimes?
Solomon hits on jealousy, being busy, and consumed with our own lives, complaining, laziness, and pride as barriers to community. Help your kids see practical ways that these make sharing life hard.

5. Let's come up with ideas for how our family can share our lives with others! What are some ideas you can think of?
Brainstorm with your children ways that your family can do things with your friends from LifeGroup, work, school, and the neighborhood. You can have a family over for dinner, host a LifeGroup cookout, go see a movie with friends, etc. Make a plan to accomplish one of these ideas in the next week and remind your children how things are an important part of sharing life with other people.

PRAY TOGETHER AS A FAMILY
Thank God that he has given you a church family to share life with. Thank Him by name for the people He has put in your life. Pray as family for those in your LifeGroup and your friends from Kidtown.

MEMORY VERSE

> "But you are a chosen race, a royal priesthood, a holy nation, a people for his own possession, that you may proclaim the excellencies of Him who call you out of darkness into his

marvelous light."

- 1 Peter 2:9

INTERACTIVE FAMILY ACTIVITY

For this week's family interactive activity we're going to compete in the Amazing Couch Cushion Tower Race! Build a large tower out of couch cushions and pillows. The tower should be small enough that one person can pick it up and carry it but big enough it's heavy and hard to balance. Build the tower on one side of your living room and use tape or toilet paper to make a finish line on the other side of the room. Get a stopwatch and play some music and you're ready to begin the race.

For the race, have each one of your children pick up the tower and time them as they move the tower past the finish line. Tell them the rules are that they cannot move the tower in pieces, they have to pick up the whole thing and balance it. If it falls over before they get to the finish line they have to rebuild it and keep going. If your kids are having fun, feel free to let them try a few times and see if they can beat their own times.

After having each child try it by themselves, put them in pairs. If you only have one child, you can be their partner. As a team do the race again. Give them a couple of tries to figure out the intricacies of balancing the tower together as a team.

When it's all over talk to them about how helpful the teamwork was in moving the Amazing Couch Cushion Tower. Ask them what was harder about working together in a team compared to doing it by themselves? Help them see the beauty of God's design for us to work together and help shoulder the load when life is heavy and hard to balance on our own.

The Good Life

WEEK 6: THE MONEY BAGS CLUB

Do kids at your school talk about who has the nicest house or the coolest clothes? It is easy to believe that our possessions define us. We often make them our identity and worth. Solomon steps in to help us see that though God wants us to enjoy what we own; we don't exist to purchase, consume, or own things.

REVIEW

On your ride home from the Gathering, ask your child the following questions:
1. What did you learn today at Kidtown?
2. What was the most fun part of today?
3. Did you meet anyone new?
4. How can we pray for your friends at Kidtown this week?

DIG DEEPER

After dinner one evening, open the Bible and lead your kids in a devotional based on the Kidtown lesson.

1. Read Ecclesiastes 5:13-16 aloud together.
- Are there any words that you don't understand in these verses?

2. In this passage Solomon says he has seen something evil. What is it?
He sees a man who spent his life trying to get more and more money and possessions, but then he loses them. Solomon asks the question, "What gain is there in chasing wealth if you can't take it with you?"

3. Read Ecclesiastes 5:19 aloud together. What does King Solomon say is a gift from God?
The ability to enjoy what He's given us, no matter how much or

how little we have. Gratitude and contentment are even bigger gifts than having money.

4. What are some gifts God has given our family that we can thank Him for?
Help prompt your kids to think of all kinds of things they can be grateful for: your house, beds, blankets, toys, stuffed animals, etc. Then push them deeper to think about the really important things in life.

INTERACTIVE FAMILY ACTIVITY

Have each of your kids go and get their most prized possession. When they bring it back, ask them to explain why it is so important to them. Then ask them what would happen if they lost that possession. Explain to them that it isn't wrong to have that possession but that in the end it doesn't make them more important to God. Teach them that God showed their worth when He died on the Cross. Possessions don't give us worth, God does:

> "For God so loved the world that He gave His only Son, that whoever believes in Him will not perish"
>
> –John 3:16

Now, reread this verse and put your child's name in place of "the world" to make it personal to them.

PRAY TOGETHER AS A FAMILY

Thank God that He meets all of our needs. Ask Him to guard your family against the lie of believing that money and possessions will make us complete. Ask Him to help your family grow in their understanding that He is the source of everlasting joy, not the things we buy.

MEMORY VERSE

"But you are a chosen race, a royal priesthood, a holy nation, a people for his own possession, that you may proclaim the excellencies of him who call you out of darkness into his marvelous light."

- 1 Peter 2:9

WEEK 7: THE FOUNTAIN OF YOUTH

Getting older terrifies most adults, but most kids don't really even think about it. The joy of youth gives us a feeling of invincibility and old age seems forever away. Solomon encourages us to embrace the reality that old age and death are coming. Facing this reality puts life into perspective and leads us to our need for Jesus.

TRAINING THOUGHTS FOR PARENTS

- Often we are afraid to talk to our kids about death because we ourselves are uncomfortable with death. Let this be a time where you grow in accepting you are getting older and are going to die someday.
- Treat getting older and death as normal. We don't need to make death too big of a deal and incredibly scary. We also don't need to make light of it or speak indirectly. We can talk realistically about it in a way that helps calm our kids down.
- Your kids may take this hard and be very scared, or they may not be fazed by this discussion at all. Some may even make weird jokes just because they don't understand it. Be prepared for any reaction.
- Prep your mind for lots of different questions your kids may want to ask: Will I die? How will I die? When will I die? Could I die tonight? Who else is going to die? What is death? Why do we have to die? Etc.- It is always okay to defer and say, "This is a conversation that we will have when you are older."
- Talk to your kids about how death is a result of sin and the fall.
- Here is an online resource that you can refer to for wisdom on talking to your kids about getting older and death: http://childrensministry.com/articles/helping-children-deal-with-death

On your ride home from the Gathering, ask your child the following questions:

1. What did you learn today at Kidtown?
2. What was the most fun part of today?
3. Did you meet anyone new?
4. How can we pray for your friends at Kidtown this week?

DIG DEEPER

After dinner one evening, open the Bible and lead your kids in a devotional based on the Kidtown lesson.

1. Read Ecclesiastes 9:1-6 aloud together.
Are there any words that you don't understand in these verses?

2. What do you think about when you think about getting old? Do you think you will like it? Why or why not? What's fun about being young? What's not great about being young? What happens to people when they get really, really old?
These are simple questions to get the conversation going and start your kids thinking about old age.

3. Interactive Family Activity:
Go outside and talk walk around with your kids. While walking, look for leaves that have fallen from the tree. Talk to your kids about why the leave has fallen from the tree (It has gotten older and died). Take this time to ask some simple but poignant questions. Here are a few to get the conversation going. 1) Have you ever known anyone who has died? 2) Why do people have to die? 3) Is there hope for us even though we know we will die? After this questions open up the Bible to Romans 6:23:

> *"For the wages of sin is death, but the gift of God is eternal life in Christ Jesus our Lord."*

This is a great opportunity to explain the Gospel and how Jesus takes away the fear of death by offering us eternal life.

4. What does death make you think of or how does death make you feel?
It's okay to be sad about death. Death is sad. Death is the result of sin in the world. God didn't originally design us to die, but because of sin we all die. That is what Romans 5:12 shows us (Read it). So death is absolutely something to be sad about.

5. Read Romans 5:21 aloud together.

> *"Sin ruled because of death. So also grace rules in the lives of those who are right with God. The grace of God brings eternal life because of what Jesus Christ our Lord has done."*

6. What good news does this verse give us about death and real life?
For believers in Jesus, death isn't the final story! Sin brought death into the world, but through his life, death, and resurrection Jesus conquers sin and death. Even though everyone will die, people who trust in Jesus will be given the gift of grace— life with God forever after this life on earth ends!

7. Why do you think it is important that we understand death?
Death reminds us that life on earth is limited. It teaches us not to waste it living for silly things, but to live for what is truly important – God and His mission. Additionally, death is a sign to us that we need a Savior. Death isn't how things are supposed to be and we need someone to make things right. Death shows us our need for Jesus and should encourage us to put our trust in Him for life with God forever after death. Death is still sad, but it's important to remember that Jesus gives us hope of life after it!

PRAY TOGETHER AS A FAMILY

Thank Jesus for the hope He gives us for life after death with God forever. Thank God that He didn't let death be the final story. Ask Him to help your family understand the reality of death, feel its sadness, but be encouraged by the hope that Jesus brings.

MEMORY VERSE

> *"Fear God and keep his commandments, for this is the whole duty of man."*
>
> - Ecclesiastes 12:13

WEEK 8: JOY, SATISFACTION, AND THE FEAR OF GOD

To summarize our study of Ecclesiastes, we'll land on Solomon's parting wisdom. *"Fear God and keep his commandments, for this is the whole duty of man."* Don't wait until you're old to love God and take Him seriously.

REVIEW

On your ride home from the Gathering, ask your child the following questions:
1. What did you learn today at Kidtown?
2. What was the most fun part of today?
3. Did you meet anyone new?
4. How can we pray for your friends at Kidtown this week?

DIG DEEPER

After dinner one evening, open the Bible and lead your kids in a devotional based on the Kidtown lesson.

1. Our family is ending our study of Ecclesiastes this week. In the last passage of Ecclesiastes, King Solomon summarizes what life is really all about.

2. Read Ecclesiastes 12:13-14 aloud together.
- Are there any words that you don't understand in these verses?
- What does Solomon say life is all about?

3. What do you think Solomon means by "fear God"?
This fear means to see God for who He truly is— the wonderful, holy, creator, King of the Universe, who is much greater than anyone in this world— and to enjoy the fact that He is involved in our lives! This is what life is all about! Pursuing and enjoying God!

4. How do you think our lives would look if this were our goal?
Because of Jesus, we know how great God is and how much He already loves and accepts us. Now we have the opportunity to enjoy Him with our whole lives. We can freely confess and repent because we know God is in control. Our fear of Him allows us to honor Jesus as King in the way we live.

5. Let's make a plan for how our family can pursue knowing God and enjoying Him together.
Parents come with ideas, but let your children contribute and then actually set up time to engage in activities that will help your whole family grow closer to God.

PRAY TOGETHER AS A FAMILY

Thank God for sending Jesus to show us who He is and save us from our sin. Thank God for the Bible that teaches about Him and His desire for our lives. Ask Him to help us live in light of the truth that He is the Great King of the Universe. Ask Him to help us get to know Him and enjoy Him.

MEMORY VERSE

"Fear God and keep his commandments, for this is the whole duty of man."

- Ecclesiastes 12:13

INTERACTIVE FAMILY ACTIVITY

Play a game we like to call, "Chief in Charge". Someone is the chief and we "follow their instructions." Each person gets to be the Chief for two minutes and during those two minutes everyone has to do whatever they do. If they do somersaults, everyone does somersaults. If they clap their hands, everyone claps their hands. The goal of the game is to keep up with the Chief. When the two minutes are up, the next person gets to be chief and the game can go on as long as you like.

Use this game to help your kids get a fun visual picture of what it looks like to follow instructions and try as hard as you can to be like the Chief – the person who is in charge.

Read Ephesians 5:1-2:

> *"You are the children that God dearly loves. So be just like him. Lead a life of love, just as Christ did. He loved us. He gave himself up for us."*

Because God loves us and because we fear God, we want to obey Him. We want to be just like Him. Just like we imitated the Chief in the game, Jesus calls us to imitate His love in our entire lives.

FAMILY PRAYER GUIDES

This prayer guide is designed to give you direction to pray for your child each day. Each prayer is accompanied with a Scripture to pray or memorize. This guide is a starting point not a checklist. Sundays are breaks from this guide as Kidtown joins you in these prayers during the Gathering. The next two months we will be covering Ecclesiastes with you. The prayers may seem repetitive but that is done on purpose so that you will be praying consistent prayers over your child.

PRAYER GUIDE: WEEK 1

MONDAY
Ecclesiastes 1:14
"I have seen all the things that are done under the sun: all of them are meaningless, a chasing after the wind."

> *Father, I pray my child chases after You and not the meaningless things of this world that can never be grasped.*

TUESDAY
Ecclesiastes 1:10-11
"I denied myself nothing my eyes desired; I refused my heart no pleasure. My heart took delight in all my work, and this was the reward for all my labor. Yet when I surveyed all that my hands had

done what I had toiled to achieve, everything was meaningless, a chasing after the wind; nothing was gained under the sun."

Father, I pray that my child is not distracted by the unfulfilling pleasure of this world. I pray that my child would not waste their life trying to find their worth in temporary rewards here on this earth but rather in heavenly rewards.

WEDNESDAY
Ecclesiastes 3:1
"There is a time for everything and a season for every activity under heaven."

Father, I pray that You would instill this truth in my child's heart. As my child goes through life's seasons I pray that they would be content in the season they are in, whether it be a season of happiness or sorrow. Help them to see Your presence and Your goodness in the midst of any circumstance. I pray that I parent in a way that is welcoming of the varying seasons of life that You may have for me.

THURSDAY
Ecclesiastes 4:4
"And I saw that all labor and all achievement spring from man's envy of his neighbor. This too is meaningless, a chasing after the wind."

Father, I pray that you would protect my child from being motivated out of envy, selfish ambition, or proud competition. Allow my child to be content in the blessings You give as the gracious giver. Help me show my contentment is in You and allow my heart not to wander into the trap of envying others.

FRIDAY
Ecclesiastes 4:9-10
"Two are better than one, because they have a good return for their work: If one falls down, his friend can help him up. But pity the man who falls and has no one to help him up!"

> *Father, community is a gracious gift You give to us. Allow my life to model being a part of a body so that my child would naturally see the beauty of living in community with others. I pray my child learns to lean on others and see Your grace through living life with others.*

SATURDAY
Ecclesiastes 4:13
"Better a poor but wise youth than an old but foolish king who no longer knows how to take warning."

> *Father, You give us warnings in life because You are a loving Father. Reveal this truth to my child's heart so discipline is seen as one of Your many forms of grace.*

PRAYER GUIDE: WEEK 2

MONDAY
Ecclesiastes 4:13
"Better a poor but wise youth than an old but foolish king who no longer knows how to take warning."

> *Father, You give us warning because You are a loving father. Reveal this truth to my child's heart so that discipline is seen as one of Your many forms of grace.*

TUESDAY
Ecclesiastes 4:9-10
"Two are better than one, because they have a good return for their work: If one falls down, his friend can help him up. But pity the man who falls and has no one to help him up!"

> *Father, community is a gracious gift You give to us. Allow my life to model being a part of the body so that my child would naturally see the beauty of living in community with others. I pray my child learns to lean on others and see Your grace through living life with others.*

WEDNESDAY
Ecclesiastes 4:4
"And I saw that all labor and all achievement spring from man's envy of his neighbor. This too is meaningless, a chasing after the wind."

> *Father, I pray that you would protect my child from being motivated out of envy, selfish ambition, or proud competition. Allow my child to be content in the blessings You give as the gracious giver. Help me show my contentment is in You and allow my heart not to wander into the trap of envying others.*

THURSDAY
Ecclesiastes 3:1
"There is a time for everything and a season for every activity under heaven."

> *Father, I pray You would instill this truth in my child's heart. As my child goes through life's seasons I pray they would be content in the season they are in, whether it be a season of happiness or*

sorrow. Help them to see Your presence and Your goodness in the midst of any circumstance. I pray I parent in a way that is welcoming of the varying seasons of life that You may have for me.

FRIDAY
Ecclesiastes 1:10-11
"I denied myself nothing my eyes desired; I refused my heart no pleasure. My heart took delight in all my work, and this was the reward for all my labor. Yet when I surveyed all that my hands had done, what I had toiled to achieve, everything was meaningless, a chasing after the wind; nothing was gained under the sun."

Father, I pray that my child is not distracted by the unfulfilling pleasure of this world. I pray that my child would not waste their life trying to find their worth in temporary rewards here on this earth but rather in heavenly rewards.

SATURDAY
Ecclesiastes 1:14
"I have seen all the things that are done under the sun: all of them are meaningless, a chasing after the wind."

Father, I pray my child chases after You and not the meaningless things of this world that can never be grasped like the wind.

PRAYER GUIDE: WEEK 3

MONDAY
Ecclesiastes 5:6
"Do not let your mouth lead you into sin."

Father, allow my child to be wise with words and realize the destructive power words can have on others. Help me be gracious in my speech towards my child so I can lovingly encourage and model this.

TUESDAY
Ecclesiastes 7:3-4
"Sorrow is better than laughter because a sad face is good for the heart. The heart of the wise is in the house of mourning, but the heart of fools is in the house of pleasure"

> Father, allow my child to know that it is okay to go to the house of mourning during certain seasons of life. Allow me to parent in a way that does not avoid sorrow but rather accepts sorrow and presses into You for Your grace during hard times. Help me to show how Your grace allows us to mourn together as a church family, but not without hope.

WEDNESDAY
Ecclesiastes 7:8
"The end of a matter is better than its beginning, and patience is better than pride."

> Father, often pride can be a huge hindrance to growing in patience. Allow my child to lean on patience through journeys rather than giving up. Lead me in patience and not pride through circumstances that may require patience.

THURSDAY
Ecclesiastes 8:7-8
"Since no man knows the future, who can tell him what is to come? No man has power over the wind to contain it; so no one has power over the day of his death."

> Father, I pray that my child would not spend precious time wor-

rying about the future but rather would put his/her trust in You because You are sovereign over all of our future.

FRIDAY
Ecclesiastes 11:7
"Light is sweet, and it pleases the eyes to see the sun."

> *Father, allow my child to discover the sweetness of life and its simple pleasure. Allow all of life's pleasures to point us toward Your incredible goodness and Your wonderful grace that You lavish upon us.*

SATURDAY
Ecclesiastes 12:1
"Remember your Creator in the days of your youth...."

> *Father, we often forget to acknowledge You especially in our busy young lives. Allow my child's youth to be marked by Your presence. Help them to live a life that doesn't ignore You as that will be detrimental to Your glory and their joy.*

PRAYER GUIDE: WEEK 4

MONDAY
Ecclesiastes 12:1
"Remember your Creator in the days of your youth...."

> *Father, we often forget to acknowledge You especially in our busy young lives. Allow my child's youth to be marked by Your presence. Help them to live a life that doesn't ignore You as that will be detrimental to Your glory and their joy.*

TUESDAY
Ecclesiastes 11:7
"Light is sweet, and it pleases the eyes to see the sun."

Father, allow my child to discover the sweetness of life and its simple pleasure. Allow all of life's pleasures to point us toward Your incredible goodness and Your incredible grace that You lavish upon us.

WEDNESDAY
Ecclesiastes 8:7-8
"Since no man knows the future, who can tell him what is to come? No man has power over the wind to contain it; so no one has power over the day of his death."

Father, I pray my child would not spend precious time worrying about the future but rather would put his/her trust in You because You are sovereign over all of our futures.

THURSDAY
Ecclesiastes 7:8
"The end of a matter is better than its beginning, and patience is better than pride."

Father, often pride can be a huge hindrance to growing in patience. Allow my child to lean on patience through journeys rather than giving up. Lead me in patience and not pride through circumstances that may require patience.

FRIDAY
Ecclesiastes 7:3-4
"Sorrow is better than laughter, because a sad face is good for the heart. The heart of the wise is in the house of mourning, but the

heart of fools is in the house of pleasure"

> *Father, allow my child to know it is okay to go to the house of mourning during certain seasons of life. Allow me to parent in a way that does not avoid sorrow but rather accepts sorrow and presses into You for Your grace during hard times. Help me to show how Your grace allows us to mourn together as a church family, but not without hope.*

SATURDAY
Ecclesiastes 5:6
"Do not let your mouth lead you into sin."

> *Father, allow my child to be wise with words and realize the destructive power words can have on others. Help me be gracious in my speech towards my child so I can lovingly encourage and model this.*

PRAYER GUIDE: WEEK 5

MONDAY
Ecclesiastes 1:14
"I have seen all the things that are done under the sun: all of them are meaningless, a chasing after the wind."

> *Father, I pray my child chases after You and not the meaningless things of this world that can never be grasped like the wind.*

TUESDAY
Ecclesiastes 5:6
"Do not let your mouth lead you into sin."

Father, allow my child to be wise with words and realize the destructive power words can have on others. Help me be gracious in my speech towards my child so I can lovingly encourage and model this.

WEDNESDAY
Ecclesiastes 3:1
"There is a time for everything and a season for every activity under heaven."

Father, I pray You would instill this truth in my child's heart. As my child goes through life's seasons I pray they would be content in the season they are in, whether it be a season of happiness or sorrow. Help them to see Your presence and Your goodness in the midst of any circumstance. I pray I parent in a way that is welcoming of the varying seasons of life that You may have for me.

THURSDAY
Ecclesiastes 7:3-4
"Sorrow is better than laughter, because a sad face is good for the heart. The heart of the wise is in the house of mourning, but the heart of fools is in the house of pleasure"

Father, allow my child to know it is okay to go to the house of mourning during certain seasons of life. Allow me to parent in a way that does not avoid sorrow but rather accepts sorrow and presses into You for Your grace during hard times. Help me to show how Your grace allows us to mourn together as a church family, but not without hope.

FRIDAY
Ecclesiastes 4:9-10

"Two are better than one, because they have a good return for their work: If one falls down, his friend can help him up. But pity the man who falls and has no one to help him up!"

Father, community is a gracious gift You give to us. Allow my life to model being a part of the body so that my child would naturally see the beauty of living in community with others. I pray my child learns to lean on others and see Your grace through living life with others.

SATURDAY
Ecclesiastes 7:8
"The end of a matter is better than its beginning, and patience is better than pride."

Father, often pride can be a huge hindrance to growing in patience. Allow my child to lean on patience through journeys rather than giving up. Lead me in patience and not pride through circumstances that may require patience.

PRAYER GUIDE: WEEK 6

MONDAY
Ecclesiastes 5:6
"Do not let your mouth lead you into sin."

Father, allow my child to be wise with words and realize the destructive power words can have on others. Help me be gracious in my speech towards my child so I can lovingly encourage and model this.

TUESDAY
Ecclesiastes 1:10-11
"I denied myself nothing my eyes desired; I refused my heart no pleasure. My heart took delight in all my work, and this was the reward for all my labor. Yet when I surveyed all that my hands had done, what I had toiled to achieve, everything was meaningless, a chasing after the wind; nothing was gained under the sun."

> *Father, I pray my child is not distracted by the unfulfilling pleasure of this world. I pray my child would not waste their life trying to find their worth in temporary rewards here on this earth but rather in heavenly rewards.*

WEDNESDAY
Ecclesiastes 7:8
"The end of a matter is better than its beginning, and patience is better than pride."

> *Father, often pride can be a huge hindrance to growing in patience. Allow my child to lean on patience through journeys rather than giving up. Lead me in patience and not pride through circumstances that may require patience.*

THURSDAY
Ecclesiastes 4:4
"And I saw that all labor and all achievement spring from man's envy of his neighbor. This too is meaningless, a chasing after the wind."

> *Father, I pray you would protect my child from being motivated out of envy, selfish ambition or proud competition. Allow my child to be content in the blessings You give as the gracious giver. Help me show my contentment is in You and allow my heart not to*

wander into the trap of envying others.

FRIDAY
Ecclesiastes 11:7
"Light is sweet, and it pleases the eyes to see the sun."

Father, allow my child to discover the sweetness of life and its simple pleasure. Allow all of life's pleasures to point us toward Your incredible goodness and Your incredible grace that You lavish upon us.

SATURDAY
Ecclesiastes 4:13
"Better a poor but wise youth than an old but foolish king who no longer knows how to take warning."

Father, You give us warning because You are a loving father, reveal this truth to my child's heart so discipline is seen as one of Your many forms of grace.

PRAYER GUIDE: WEEK 7

MONDAY
Ecclesiastes 3:1
"There is a time for everything and a season for every activity under heaven."

Father, I pray You would instill this truth in my child's heart. As my child goes through life's seasons I pray they would be content in the season they are in, whether it be a season of happiness or sorrow. Help them to see Your presence and Your goodness in the midst of any circumstance. I pray I parent in a way that is welcoming of the varying seasons of life You may have for me.

TUESDAY
Ecclesiastes 7:3-4
"Sorrow is better than laughter, because a sad face is good for the heart. The heart of the wise is in the house of mourning, but the heart of fools is in the house of pleasure"

> *Father, allow my child to know it is okay to go to the house of mourning during certain seasons of life. Allow me to parent in a way that does not avoid sorrow but rather accepts sorrow and presses into You for Your grace during hard times. Help me to show how Your grace allows us to mourn together as a church family, but not without hope.*

WEDNESDAY
Ecclesiastes 5:6
"Do not let your mouth lead you into sin."

> *Father, allow my child to be wise with words and realize the destructive power words can have on others. Help me be gracious in my speech towards my child so I can lovingly encourage and model this.*

THURSDAY
Ecclesiastes 8:7-8
"Since no man knows the future, who can tell him what is to come? No man has power over the wind to contain it; so no one has power over the day of his death."

> *Father, I pray my child would not spend precious time worrying about the future but rather would put his/her trust in You because*

You are sovereign over all of our future.

FRIDAY
Ecclesiastes 4:9-10
"Two are better than one, because they have a good return for their work: If one falls down, his friend can help him up. But pity the man who falls and has no one to help him up!"

> *Father, community is a gracious gift You give to us. Allow my life to model being a part of a body so my child would naturally see the beauty of living in community with others. I pray my child learns to lean on others and see Your grace through living life with others.*

SATURDAY
Ecclesiastes 12:1
"Remember your Creator in the days of your youth...."

> *Father, we often forget to acknowledge You especially in our busy young lives. Allow my child's youth to be marked by Your presence. Help them to live a life that doesn't ignore You as that will be detrimental to Your glory and their joy.*

PRAYER GUIDE: WEEK 8

MONDAY
Ecclesiastes 12:1
"Remember your Creator in the days of your youth...."

> *Father, we often forget to acknowledge You especially in our busy young lives. Allow my child's youth to be marked by Your presence. Help them to live a life that doesn't ignore You as that will be detrimental to Your glory and their joy.*

TUESDAY
Ecclesiastes 11:7
"Light is sweet, and it pleases the eyes to see the sun."

Father, allow my child to discover the sweetness of life and its simple pleasure. Allow all of life's pleasures to point us toward Your incredible goodness and Your incredible grace You lavish upon us.

WEDNESDAY
Ecclesiastes 8:7-8
"Since no man knows the future, who can tell him what is to come? No man has power over the wind to contain it; so no one has power over the day of his death."

Father, I pray my child would not spend precious time worrying about the future but rather would put his/her trust in You because You are sovereign over all of our future.

THURSDAY
Ecclesiastes 1:10-11
"I denied myself nothing my eyes desired; I refused my heart no pleasure. My heart took delight in all my work, and this was the reward for all my labor. Yet when I surveyed all that my hands had done what I had toiled to achieve, everything was meaningless, a chasing after the wind; nothing was gained under the sun."

Father, I pray my child is not distracted by the unfulfilling pleasure of this world. I pray my child would not waste their life trying to find their worth in temporary rewards here on this earth but rather in heavenly rewards.

FRIDAY
Ecclesiastes 7:3-4

"Sorrow is better than laughter, because a sad face is good for the heart. The heart of the wise is in the house of mourning, but the heart of fools is in the house of pleasure"

> *Father, allow my child to know it is okay to go to the house of mourning during certain seasons of life. Allow me to parent in a way that does not avoid sorrow but rather accepts sorrow and presses into You for Your grace during hard times. Help me to show how Your grace allows us to mourn together as a church family, but not without hope.*

SATURDAY
Ecclesiastes 7:8

"The end of a matter is better than its beginning, and patience is better than pride."

> *Father, often pride can be a huge hindrance to growing in patience. Allow my child to lean on patience through journeys rather than giving up. Lead me in patience and not pride through circumstances that may require patience.*

APPENDICES

APPENDIX A
THE SOLOMON CLUB

The Solomon Club is a fictitious club made up of current celebrities and historical figures who have come to some of the same realizations that Solomon came to regarding how meaningless our pursuits are under the sun. We've included a series of quotes from the Solomon Club including a Top Ten (these quotes make it sound like the celebrity has been studying Ecclesiastes or something) and a series of Solomon Club quotes that go with each chapter of this study.

TOP TEN:

Brad Pitt

> "I know all these things are ... important to us - the car, the condo, our version of success - but ... I say we gotta find something else. The emphasis now is on success and personal gain. I'm sitting in it, and I'm telling you, that's not it. I'm the guy who's got everything. And I'm telling you, once you've got everything, then you're just left with yourself: it doesn't help you sleep any better, and you don't wake up any better because of it."

Brad Pitt agrees with Solomon. Success doesn't lead to the Good Life.

Jim Carrey

> "I wish everyone could get rich and famous and everything they ever dreamed of so they can see that's not the answer."

Jim Carrey agrees with Solomon. Having everything you've ever wanted doesn't deliver the Good Life.

Madonna

> "My drive in life comes from a fear of being mediocre. That is always pushing me. I push past one spell of it and discover myself as a special human being but then I feel I am still mediocre and uninteresting unless I do something else. Because even though I have become somebody, I still have to prove that I am somebody. My struggle has never ended and I guess it never will."

Madonna agrees with Solomon. Doing something special doesn't deliver the Good Life.

Tom Brady

> "Why do I have three Super Bowl rings and still think there's something greater out there for me? I mean, maybe a lot of people would say, 'Hey man, this is what is.' I reached my goal, my dream, my life. Me, I think, 'God, it's got to be more than this.' I mean this isn't, this can't be what it's all cracked up to be."

Tom Brady agrees with Solomon. Accomplishments don't deliver the Good Life.

Marilyn Monroe

> A sex symbol becomes a thing. I hate being a thing. Being a sex symbol is a heavy load to carry, especially when one is tired, hurt and bewildered. Hollywood is a place where they'll pay you $50,000 for a kiss and 50 cents for your soul.

Marilyn Monroe agrees with Solomon. Being desired by every man on earth doesn't lead to the Good Life.

Van Morrison

> Being famous was extremely disappointing for me. When I became famous it was a complete drag and it is still a complete drag.

Van Morrison agrees with Solomon. Fame doesn't lead to the Good Life.

Natalie Portman

> There's always pressure, from other people and yourself. If you're happy with the looks you're born with, then what are you going to do your whole life? We keep thinking up new things and finding better ways of doing things because we're not happy with what we're given.

Natalie Portman agrees with Solomon. The Good Life keeps escaping us.

Dustin Hoffman

> One thing about being successful is that I stopped being afraid of dying. Once you're a star you're dead already. You're embalmed.

Dustin Hoffman agrees with Solomon. Success doesn't deliver the Good Life.

Ben Affleck

> I'm not the type of guy who enjoys one-night stands. It leaves me feeling very empty and cynical. It's not even fun sexually.

Ben Affleck agrees with Solomon. Pleasure and sex don't deliver the Good Life.

John D. Rockefeller

> I have made millions, but they have brought me no happiness.

John D. Rockefeller agrees with Solomon. Money doesn't lead to the Good Life.

HONORABLE MENTIONS:

Jude Law

> We all have times when we go home at night and pull out our hair and feel misunderstood and lonely and like we're falling. I think the brain is such that there is always going to be something missing.

Jude Law agrees with Solomon. Nothing on earth leads to the Good Life.

Aldous Huxley

> Your true traveller finds boredom rather agreeable than painful. It is the symbol of his liberty - his excessive freedom. He accepts his boredom, when it comes, not merely philosophically, but almost with pleasure.

Aldous Huxley agrees with Solomon. Accepting boredom is part of the Good Life.

Charlie Sheen

> [The drugs] bored the hell out of me after a while."

Charlie Sheen agrees with Solomon. Epic parties don't lead to the Good Life.

Benjamin Franklin

> Many a man thinks he is buying pleasure, when he is really selling himself to it.

Benjamin Franklin agrees with Solomon. Pleasure doesn't lead to the Good Life.

F. Scott Fitzgerald

> Life is essentially a cheat and its conditions are those of defeat; the redeeming things are not happiness and pleasure but the deeper satisfactions that come out of struggle.

F. Scott Fitzgerald agrees with Solomon. Pleasure doesn't lead to the Good Life.

Dustin Hoffman

> One thing about being successful is that I stopped being afraid of dying. Once you're a star you're dead already. You're embalmed.

Dustin Hoffman agrees with Solomon. Success doesn't lead to the Good Life.

Albert Einstein

> Try not to become a man of success, but rather try to become a man of value.

Albert Einstein agrees with Solomon. Success doesn't lead to the Good Life.

Bill Gates

> Success is a lousy teacher. It seduces smart people into thinking they can't lose.

Bill Gates agrees with Solomon. Success doesn't lead to the Good Life.

Emily Dickinson

> Success is counted sweetest by those who never succeed.

Emily Dickinson agrees with Solomon. Success doesn't lead to the Good Life.

Katharine Hepburn

> Death will be a great relief. No more interviews.

Katharine Hepburn agrees with Solomon. Success doesn't lead to the Good Life.

Mahatma Gandhi

> I do not want to foresee the future. I am concerned with taking care of the present. God has given me no control over the moment following.

Mahatma Gandhi agrees with Solomon. The illusion of control doesn't lead to the Good Life.

John Steinbeck

> Life is a journey much like marriage. The certain way to be wrong is to think you control it.

John Steinbeck agrees with Solomon. The illusion of control doesn't lead to the Good Life.

Albert Einstein

> It is strange to be known so universally and yet to be so lonely.

Albert Einstein agrees with Solomon. Famous and lonely doesn't lead to the Good Life.

Judy Garland

> If I'm such a legend, then why am I so lonely? Let me tell you, legends are all very well if you've got somebody around who loves you.

Judy Garland agrees with Solomon. Famous and lonely doesn't lead to the Good Life.

Mother Teresa

> The most terrible poverty is loneliness, and the feeling of be-

ing unloved."

Mother Teresa agrees with Solomon. Independence doesn't lead to the Good Life.

Benjamin Franklin

> Money has never made man happy, nor will it, there is nothing in its nature to produce happiness. The more of it one has the more one wants.

Benjamin Franklin agrees with Solomon. Money doesn't lead to the Good Life.

Henry Ford

> A business that makes nothing but money is a poor business. I was happier when doing a mechanic's job.

Henry Ford agrees with Solomon. Money doesn't lead to the Good Life.

W.H. Vanderbilt

> The care of $200 milllion is enough to kill anyone. There is no pleasure in it.

W.H. Vanderbilt agrees with Solomon. Money doesn't lead to the Good Life.

John D. Rockefeller

> I have made millions, but they have brought me no happiness.

John D. Rockefeller agrees with Solomon. Money doesn't lead to the Good Life.

Andrew Carnegie

> Millionaires seldom smile.

Andrew Carnegie agrees with Solomon. Money doesn't lead to the Good Life.

Woody Allen

> It's not that I'm afraid to die. I just don't want to be there when it happens.

Woody Allen agrees with Solomon. Escaping life doesn't lead to the Good Life.

Steve Jobs

> No one wants to die. Even people who want to go to heaven don't want to die to get there. And yet death is the destination we all share. No one has ever escaped it. And that is as it should be, because Death is very likely the single best invention of Life. It is Life's change agent. It clears out the old to make way for the new.

Steve Jobs agrees with Solomon. Staying young forever doesn't lead to the Good Life.

Marilyn Monroe

> I want to grow old without facelifts... I want to have the courage to be loyal to the face I've made. Sometimes I think it would be easier to avoid old age, to die young, but then

you'd never complete your life, would you? You'd never wholly know you."

Marilyn Monroe agrees with Solomon. Staying young forever doesn't lead to the Good Life.

Andy Rooney

"It's paradoxical that the idea of living a long life appeals to everyone, but the idea of getting old doesn't appeal to anyone."

Andy Rooney agrees with Solomon. Staying young forever doesn't lead to the Good Life.

Lawrence Welk

Never trust anyone completely but God. Love people, but put your full trust only in God.

Lawrence Welk agrees with Solomon. God alone leads to the Good Life.

Henry Ford

I believe God is managing affairs and that He doesn't need any advice from me. With God in charge, I believe everything will work out for the best in the end. So what is there to worry about.

Henry Ford agrees with Solomon. God alone leads to the Good Life.

Jesus

> Do not let your hearts be troubled. Trust in God; trust also in me.

Jesus agrees with Solomon. God alone leads to the Good Life.

Jimmy Dean

> God is bigger than people think.

Jimmy Dean agrees with Solomon. Fear of God leads to the Good Life.

Jesus

> I tell you, my friends, do not fear those who kill the body, and after that have nothing more that they can do. But I will warn you whom to fear: fear him who, after he has killed, has authority to cast into hell. Yes, I tell you, fear him!

Jesus agrees with Solomon. Fear of God leads to the Good Life.

Benjamin Franklin

> Wine is constant proof that God loves us and loves to see us happy.

Benjamin Franklin agrees with Solomon. God alone gives the Good Life.

APPENDIX B
INTERPRETIVE DIFFICULTIES

A few months ago, I read a simple tweet from a Midtown family member composed of a single hashtag: #NotClearOnEcclesiastes. My excitement about our upcoming campaign started to grow. To many Christians, Ecclesiastes is a very strange read. Throughout the book, Solomon often sounds depressed, incredibly cynical and at times he seems to say blatantly untrue things or Biblically false ideas. On top of all of that, there are times when he seems to contradict himself.

But hiding behind these initial frustrations and confusions lies a wealth of wisdom, insight and truth waiting for us. When we understand the literary genre and the nature of the task Solomon is accomplishing throughout Ecclesiastes, the light bulbs start to turn on with otherwise very dark passages. Wisdom literature graces us with some of the most helpful, beautiful passages in all of Scripture and simultaneously befuddles us with some of the most confusing passages in all of Scripture.

And Ecclesiastes is a very unique example of wisdom literature. Proverbs, Psalms and Song of Solomon are fairly straight forward examples of wisdom literature in that they are consistently proclaiming truths about God and general truths about the universe. Job and Ecclesiastes are less direct in their approach. Job asks the deep questions of life from the perspective of a man who literally lost everything. Ecclesiastes asks the deep questions of life from the perspective of a man who literally gained everything. Considered together, the two books provide an incredible testimony to life satisfaction and meaning being found in God alone… both in the midst of incredible suffering and in the midst of incredible affluence.

When it comes to reading the actual text of wisdom literature, much of the confusion is simplified just by understanding that wisdom literature often speaks in broad generalizations – sweeping truisms that try to explain aspects of the universe that frequently hold true under normal circumstances. Elizabeth Achtemeier explains:

"Out of all of the chaos of experience, Wisdom finds customary 'orders' in the world – ways in which human beings and natural phenomena ordinarily behave. It's aim, then, is to teach men and women these 'orders,' so they may know how to act in harmony with the world around them."

Job, Proverbs, the Psalms, Ecclesiastes, Song of Songs and portions of James present us with wide sweeping observations that seek to explain common rhythms and patterns in the human experience. Much of the confusion comes from attempting to over apply an overarching truism from wisdom literature to a highly specific scenario in our own daily experience. Because wisdom literature deals with larger truisms, it can also seem to be self-contradictory. A classic example is Proverbs 26:4-5:

> *"Answer not a fool according to his folly, lest you be like him yourself. Answer a fool according to his folly, lest he be wise in his own eyes."*

Certainly these two sentences contradict each other, right? Well, no. Not if you understand their purpose. In v. 4, the instruction is, "Do not answer a fool according to his folly, or you will get dragged down into his foolish manner of argument." He's talking about trolling. Fools often dangle a silly argument as bait, lobbing it out there specifically with the purpose of enticing others into an argument that ends up being a foolish (oftentimes angry) waste of time. This is easily observed constantly on the internet in facebook and blog comment sections. However in v. 5, we are instructed to answer a fool according to his folly lest he think himself wise. The different instruction is that at times, it is wise to expose a fool's foolishness so that he doesn't believe himself to be wise and continue spouting his destructive thinking.

So both statements are true. Sometimes, it is wise to avoid an argument with a fool that would be a waste of your time and theirs (especially if the issue is insignificant). At other times, it is wise to engage and expose a fool's foolishness to prevent his foolishness form having negative impact on others. How do I know which one to do? Discernment. The wisdom literature's purpose isn't to tell us exactly what to do in each and every situation. It's goal is to give us broad rules to help us be able to discern well and respond to individual situations in light of broader wisdom.

Even within the wisdom literature subset, Ecclesiastes still presents some unique challenges. Solomon commends wisdom in Ecclesiastes like he does in Proverbs; however, he approaches it from a very different angle. While Proverbs takes a high view of wisdom, teaching us how to be successful in the real world, Ecclesiastes deals with the deeper questions of our meaning, purpose and role in the universe. Addressing these more profound issues of the uncertainties of human experience, Solomon's attitude toward wisdom in Ecclesiastes is surprising. Rather than speaking of wisdom with lasting high value, he speaks of it as only a short-term advantage.

"Both fool and wise die, rendering void the benefits of wisdom."

The reason for Solomon's apparent pessimism throughout the book of Ecclesiastes that we also unpacked in the introduction letter originates from the nature of the task that he is accomplishing for us. Throughout the book, Solomon walks in a tension of two views of life:

1. Life with no view of God.
2. Life with God in view.

Solomon spends a majority of Ecclesiastes considering view number 1 which is why it tends to be so pessimistic, cynical and strange sounding. In brief moments throughout the book he expands his view to include God and we get breaths of fresh air. Whenever you find yourself stumped by a verse or a passage in Ecclesiastes, immediately ask yourself the question "Is he describing life with no view of God right now?" This is the case almost every time he is depressed sounding or seemingly wrong.

For example in Ecclesiastes 10:19, Solomon writes:

"Money answers everything."

At first glance that is blatantly wrong. But here he is describing life with no view of God and saying at a practical level, money is an answer to an incredible amount of problems under the sun. It won't fix the underlying brokenness but it can certain solve a lot of symptomatic issues. It's a truism presented in a very specific context of life considered with no view of God.

PRACTICAL STEPS TO INTERPRETING ECCLESIASTES:

1. Spend time praying and meditating on the tough passages asking the Holy Spirit to illuminate them to you.
2. Ask yourself the question, "Is he describing life with no view of God right now?"
3. If you are still stuck, talk to your LG and see if you can figure

it out together.
4. In a pinch, consult commentaries, your LG coach or someone you know with more biblical knowledge.
5. Don't let a confusing statement here or there and a seemingly pessimistic tone limit you from enjoying all that Jesus has to offer us in this book. When it's the hardest to understand, rely on Jesus' strength the most. When it seems too murky to press on, pray for Jesus' light to illuminate it. And together as a family, let's learn from Jesus through Solomon how to live the good life.

APPENDIX C
EXTRA RESOURCES

BOOKS:
When the Game Is Over, It All Goes Back In the Box
John Ortberg

Every Good Endeavor
Timothy Keller

Preaching Christ from Ecclesiastes
Sydney Greidanus

The Beginning and End of Wisdom
Douglas O'Donell

The Book of Ecclesiastes
Tremper Longman

SERMON SERIES:
Ecclesiastes
By: Matt Chandler
July – December 2006.
http://www.thevillagechurch.net/resources/sermons/#series-sort_ecclesiastes

Ecclesiastes
Mark Driscoll
March – August 2003.
http://marshill.com/media/ecclesiastes

The Pursuit
Darrin Patrick
April – June 2012
http://thejourney.org/media/pursuit

www.ingramcontent.com/pod-product-compliance
Lightning Source LLC
Chambersburg PA
CBHW050954050426
42337CB00051B/838